JOYFUL origami BOXES

TOMOKO FUSE

JAPAN PUBLICATIONS TRADING COMPANY

Published by Japan Publications Trading Co., Ltd.,
  1-2-1 Sarugaku-cho, Chiyoda-ku, Tokyo, 101-0064 Japan

First edition, First printing: March 1996
              Second printing: March 1997
              Third printing: March 1999

Distributors:

United States: Kodansha America, Inc. through Oxford University Press,
  198 Madison Avenue, New York, NY 10016.
Canada: Fitzhenry & Whiteside Ltd.,
  195 Allstate Parkway, Markham, Ontario L3R 4T8.
United Kingdom and Europe: Premier Book Marketing Ltd.,
  1 Gower Street, London WC1E 6HA, England.
Australia and New Zealand: Bookwise International,
  54 Crittenden Road, Findon, South Australia 5023, Australia.
The Far East and Japan: Japan Publications Trading Co., Ltd.,
  1-2-1 Sarugaku-cho, Chiyoda-ku, Tokyo, 101-0064 Japan.

10 9 8 7 6 5 4 3

ISBN 0-87040-974-3

Printed in Japan

CONTENTS

Origami creations are usually made from one piece of square paper but unit origami is different. It is made up of several units of folded paper, which are joined together without the use of paste. Folding these units is very easy and the method of joining them is very interesting, just like solving a puzzle. It is delightful and wonderful when unexpected intricate patterns appear in the completed works.

Presented in this book are triangle, square, octagon, heptagon, hexagon boxes, and variations like flowery plates. The same units can be made to show different patterns if the method of joining is changed. It is like looking into a kaleidoscope. Now let's start making boxes, imagining the things to be put in, color schemes, and the completed shapes. The handsome boxes have charm that bring peace of mind and happiness.

January 15, 1996

Tomoko Fuse

List of Illustrations

clockwise from top : Flowery Plate （p.60）, Triangle Box （pp.22,24）, Square Box C （p.39）, Pyramid Lid with a Ribbon （p.29）.

clockwise from top : Octagon Double Pinwheel (p.71), Octagon Box (p.76), Hexagon Steeple-crowned Cap (p.94), Flowery Plate (p.60), Tray with stand (p.19)

from top to bottom : Pyramid Lid ⟨p.27⟩, Docking Box 2 ⟨p.18⟩, Heart-shaped Flowery Plates ⟨p.63⟩.

from top to bottom : Docking Box 1-B (p.17), Octagon Box,variation (p.72), Square Box D (p.41), Square Box E (p.49).

top : Hexagon Starry Pinwheel（p.91）. *bottom from left to right :* Square Box E´with Small Plate（pp.50,55）,
Square Box E˝（p.51）, Square Box A,mixed assembly（p.33）, Square Box 1（p.43）.

clockwise from top : Heptagon Double Pinwheel（p.84）, Heptagon Starry Pinwheel（p.81）, Heptagon Box（p.82）, Octagon Flowery Pinwheel（p.65）, Square Box 2（p.45）, Square Box A-a（p.34）.

Symbols

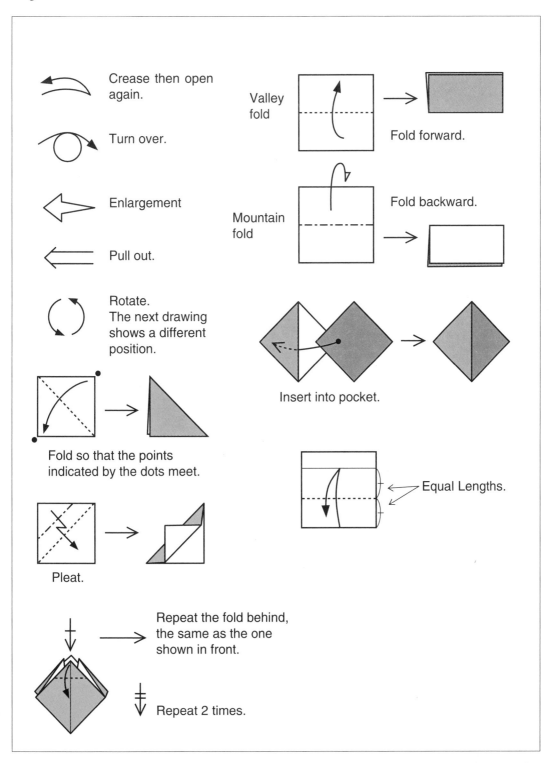

Crease then open again.

Turn over.

Enlargement

Pull out.

Rotate.
The next drawing shows a different position.

Fold so that the points indicated by the dots meet.

Pleat.

Repeat the fold behind, the same as the one shown in front.

Repeat 2 times.

Valley fold

Fold forward.

Mountain fold

Fold backward.

Insert into pocket.

Equal Lengths.

Docking Box *1*

**A simple and easy box folded from 2 pieces of paper.
If you add in one more fold, you will get Box B.**

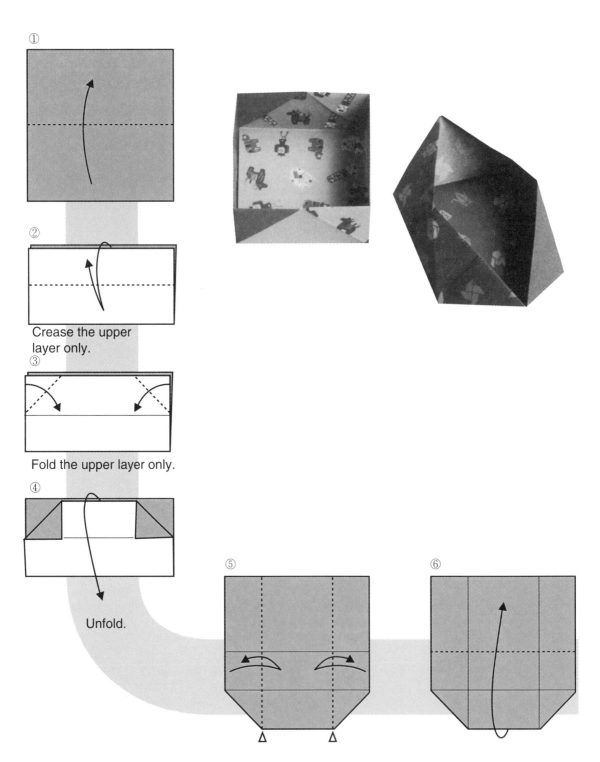

①

② Crease the upper layer only.

③ Fold the upper layer only.

④ Unfold.

⑤

⑥

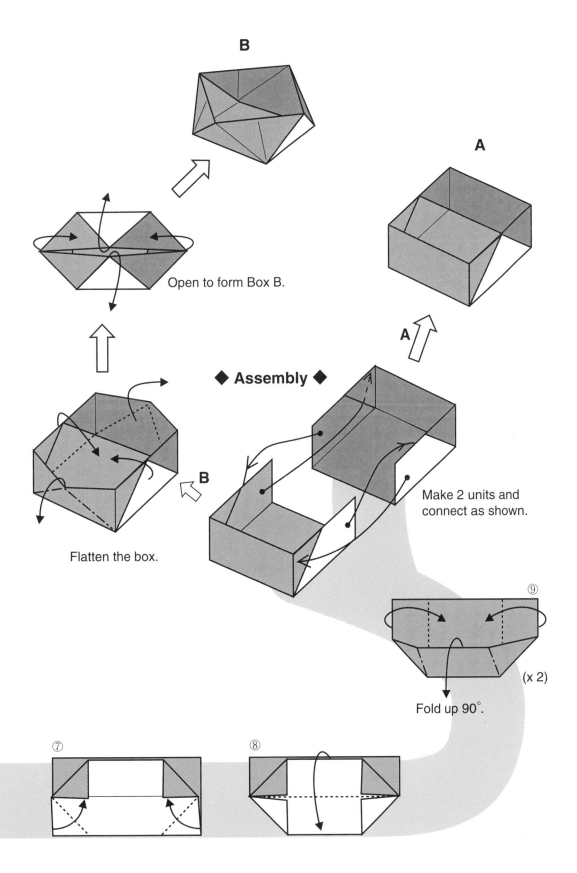

B

Open to form Box B.

A

◆ Assembly ◆

A

Flatten the box.

B

Make 2 units and
connect as shown.

⑨

(x 2)

Fold up 90°.

⑦

⑧

Docking Box 2

With a piece of rectangular paper.

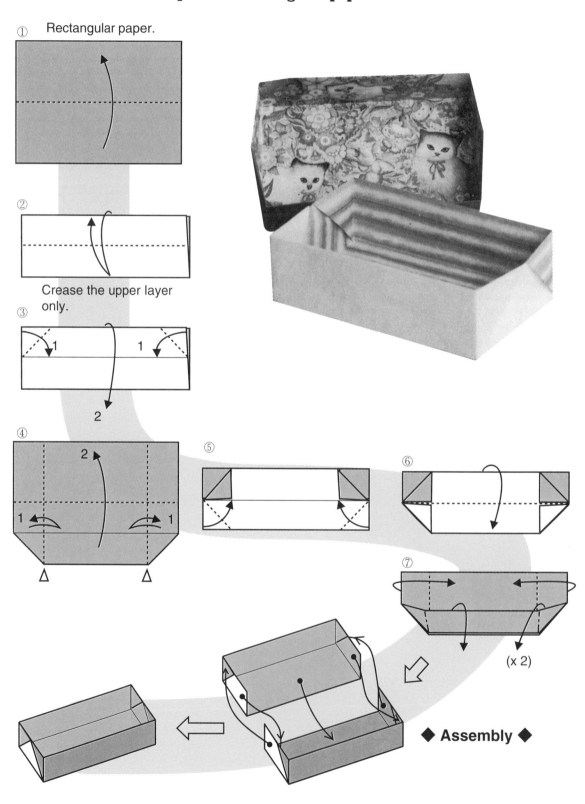

① Rectangular paper.

② Crease the upper layer only.

③

④

⑤

⑥

⑦ (x 2)

◆ Assembly ◆

Tray with Stand

A tray with tall stand. By changing folding lines as shown on the next page, you can change the height of the stand and size of the box.

Rectangular papers can also be used.

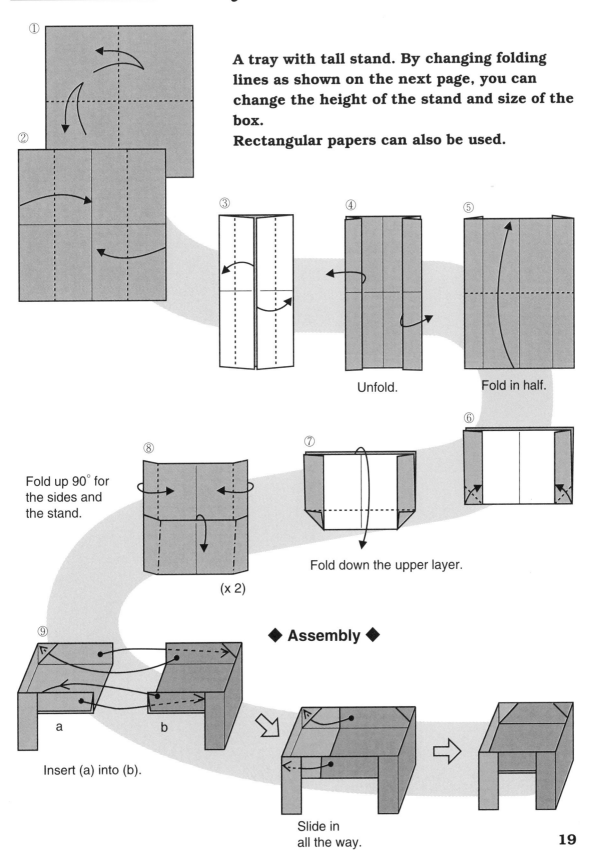

①

②

③

④ Unfold.

⑤ Fold in half.

⑥

⑦ Fold down the upper layer.

⑧ Fold up 90° for the sides and the stand. (x 2)

◆ Assembly ◆

⑨ Insert (a) into (b).

a   b

Slide in all the way.

── VARIATION ──

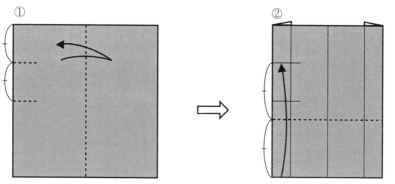

①

④

Fold as in steps ②-④ on page 19.

②

③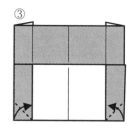

Fold and assemble the same way as steps ⑦-⑨ on page 19.

RECTANGULAR PAPER

(Short sideways)

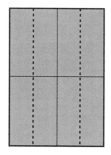

(Long sideways)

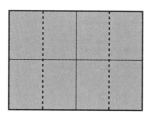

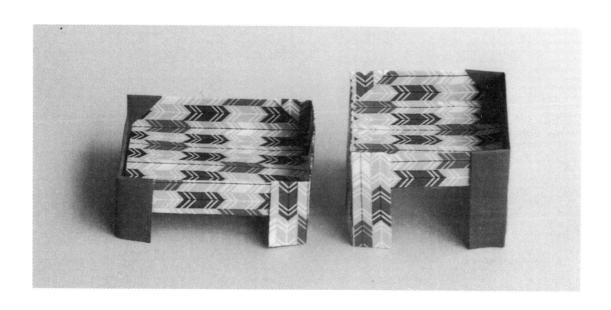

Triangle Box - *Body*

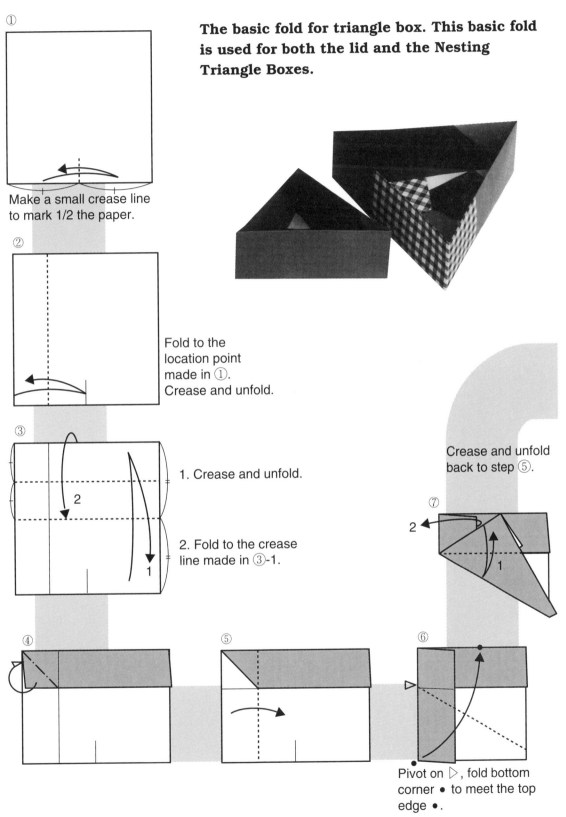

① Make a small crease line to mark 1/2 the paper.

The basic fold for triangle box. This basic fold is used for both the lid and the Nesting Triangle Boxes.

② Fold to the location point made in ①. Crease and unfold.

③
1. Crease and unfold.

2. Fold to the crease line made in ③-1.

Crease and unfold back to step ⑤.

⑦
2

1

④

⑤

⑥
Pivot on ▷, fold bottom corner • to meet the top edge •.

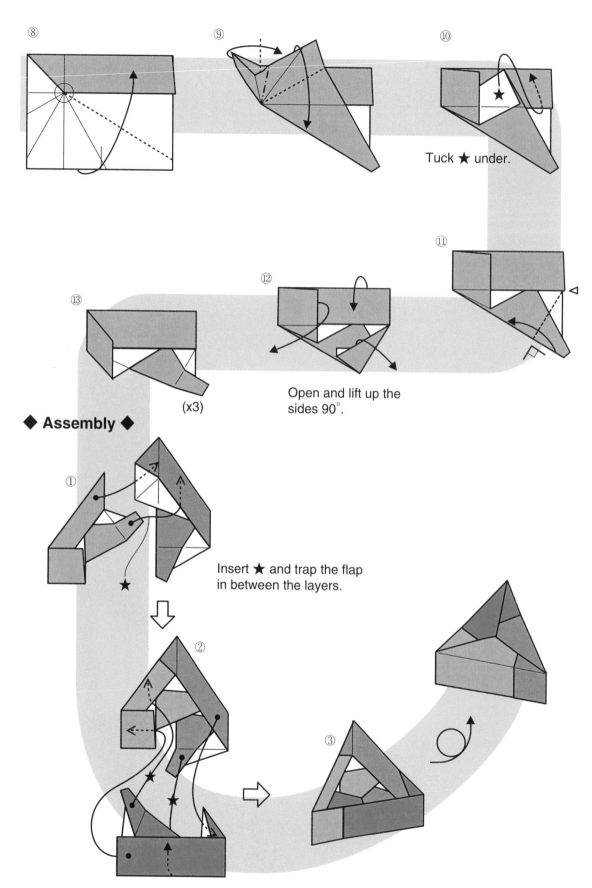

⑧

⑨

⑩

Tuck ★ under.

⑪

⑫

⑬

Open and lift up the
sides 90°.

(x3)

◆ **Assembly** ◆

①

Insert ★ and trap the flap
in between the layers.

②

③

Triangle Box - *Lid*

The length L determines the size of the box. The side of the lid is 2 to 3 mm longer than that of the body. Use the first paper as a template for the second and third paper.

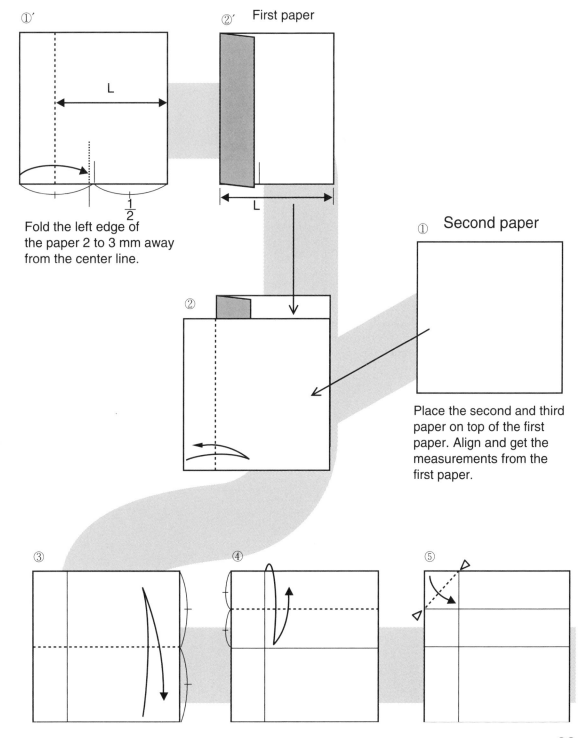

①′

L

$\frac{1}{2}$

Fold the left edge of the paper 2 to 3 mm away from the center line.

②′ First paper

L

② Second paper

Place the second and third paper on top of the first paper. Align and get the measurements from the first paper.

②

③

④

⑤

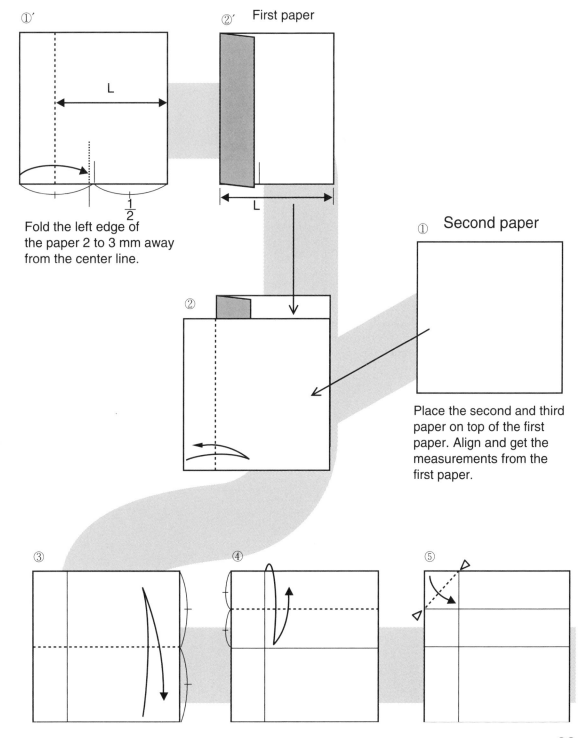

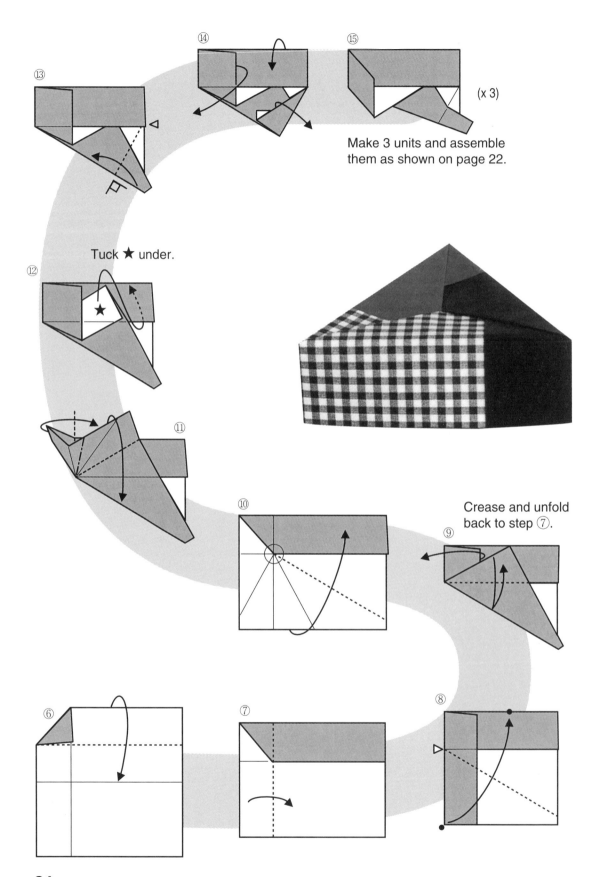

⑭ ⑬ ⑮

(x 3)

Make 3 units and assemble
them as shown on page 22.

Tuck ★ under.

⑫

⑪

Crease and unfold
back to step ⑦.

⑩ ⑨

⑥ ⑦ ⑧

Nesting Triangle Boxes

By changing the length of L, you can make a series of boxes, each one smaller than the previous.
The maximum width of the folded flap (a) is 1/3 of the side. It is possible to make 5 or 6 nesting boxes.

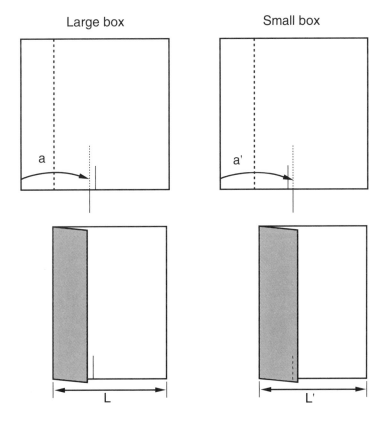

Large box   Small box

Pyramid Lid

Make the lid fit the body of the box on page 21.

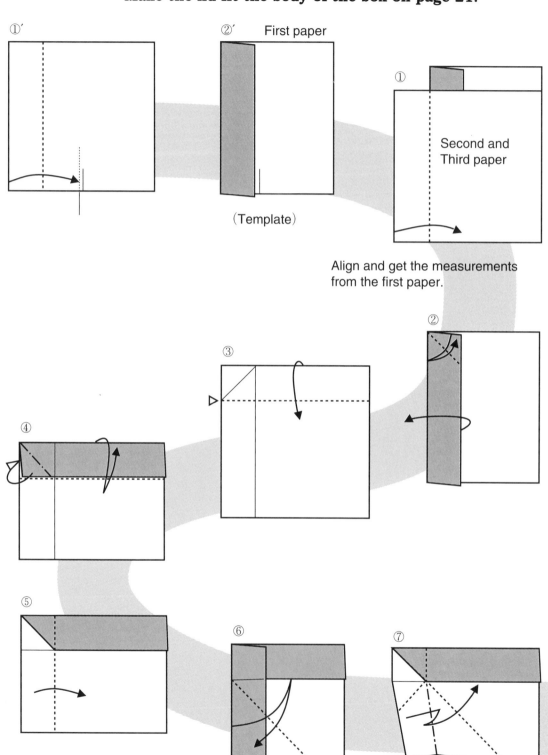

①′

②′　First paper

(Template)

①　Second and Third paper

Align and get the measurements from the first paper.

②

③

④

⑤

⑥

⑦

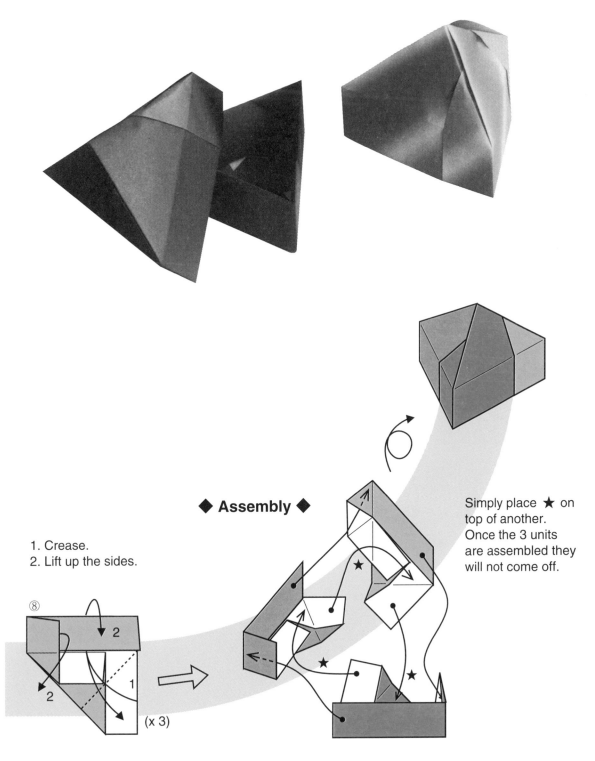

◆ **Assembly** ◆

1. Crease.
2. Lift up the sides.

Simply place ★ on top of another. Once the 3 units are assembled they will not come off.

⑧

2

1

2

(x 3)

Pyramid Lid with a Ribbon

The lid has a ribbon on top.

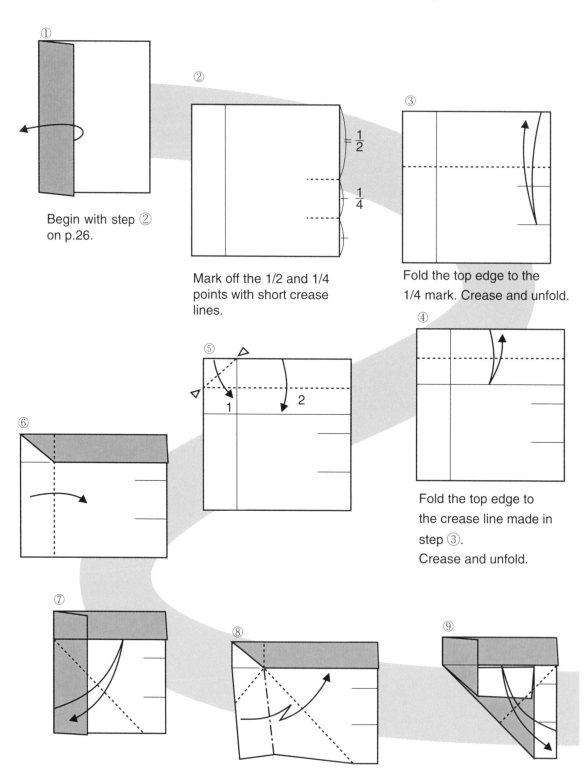

① Begin with step ② on p.26.

② Mark off the 1/2 and 1/4 points with short crease lines.

③ Fold the top edge to the 1/4 mark. Crease and unfold.

④ Fold the top edge to the crease line made in step ③.
Crease and unfold.

Note location points.
(• to meet •)

⑩

⑪

(x 3)

Square Box A

You can get various patterns by joining
the same units differently.
Some boxes will look more attractive if you make them
with the colors on the bottom or inside.
(example as shown in (b))

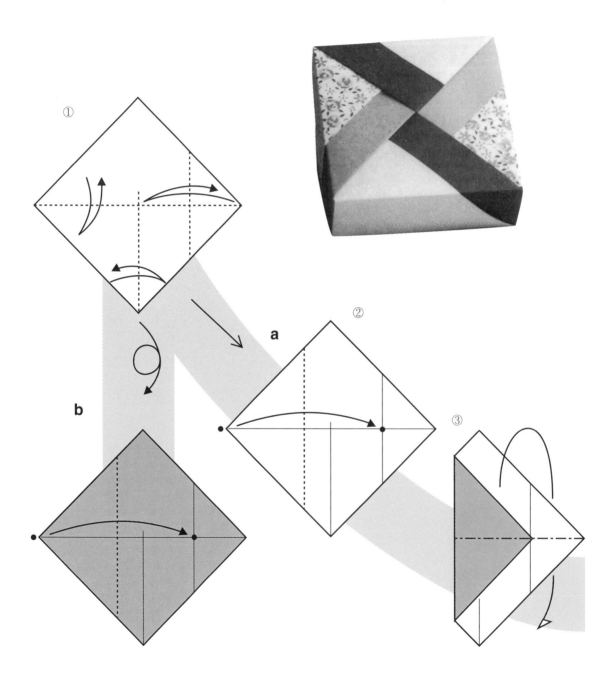

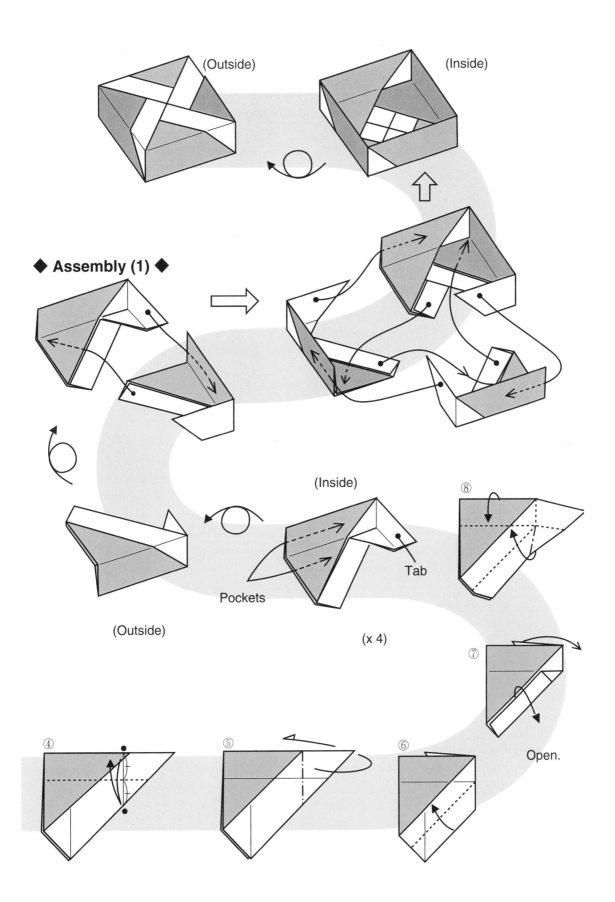

(Outside)

(Inside)

◆ **Assembly (1)** ◆

(Inside)

Tab

Pockets

(Outside)

(x 4)

⑧

⑦

Open.

④

⑤

⑥

31

Changing the Assembly

Let's change the joining of (A).

Begin with step (b) on page 30.

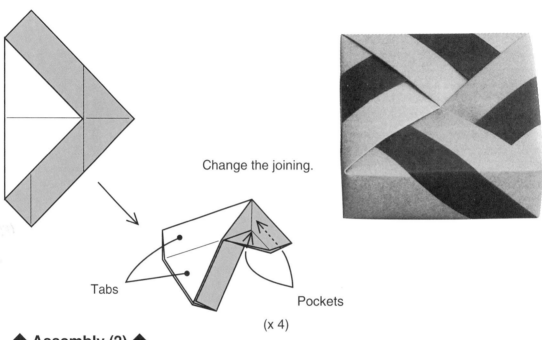

Change the joining.

Tabs

Pockets

(x 4)

◆ Assembly (2) ◆

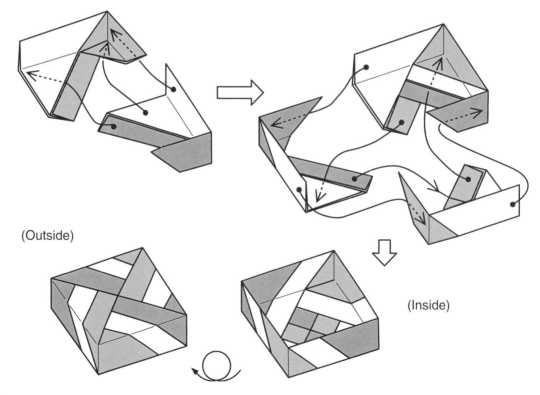

(Outside)

(Inside)

Mixed Assembly

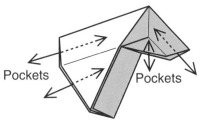

Pockets

Pockets

The unit (A) has two pockets, right and left and you can insert tabs into either of them. Experiment with the different ways of joining.

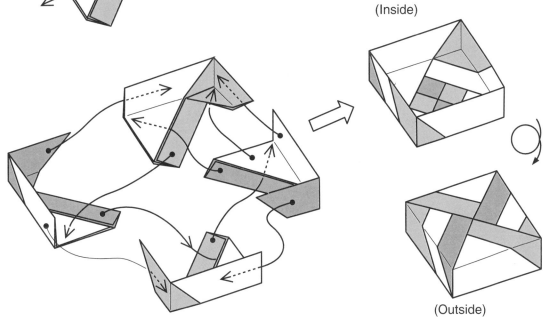

(Inside)

(Outside)

Variation of Square Box A

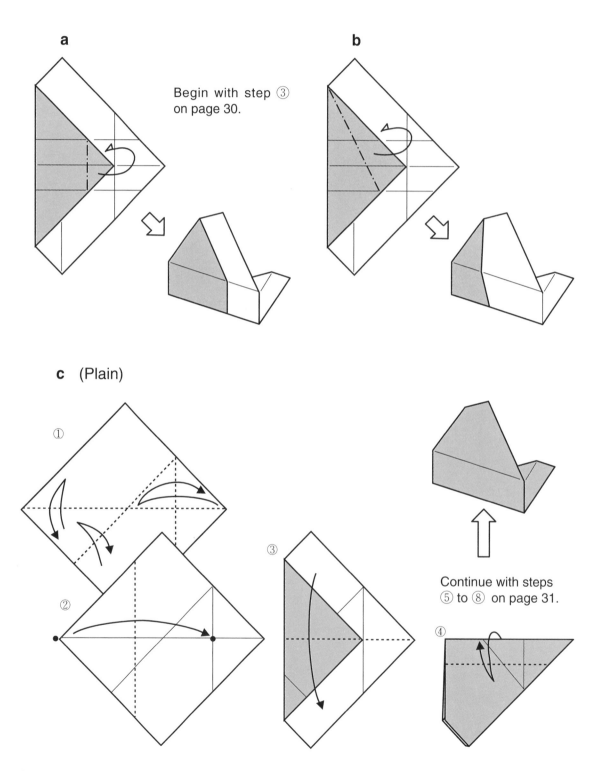

a

Begin with step ③ on page 30.

b

c (Plain)

①

②

③

④

Continue with steps ⑤ to ⑧ on page 31.

Pyramid Lid with a Ribbon (p.28)

Nesting Triangle Boxes (p.25)

Flowery Plate (p.58)

Square Box A variation (p.34)

Square Box A variation (p.34)

Square Box A variation (p.34)

35

Square Box B

Begin with step ③ of (b) on page 30.

By changing the folds of the unit of Square Box (A), the patterns of Assembly (2) on page 32 will be reversed.

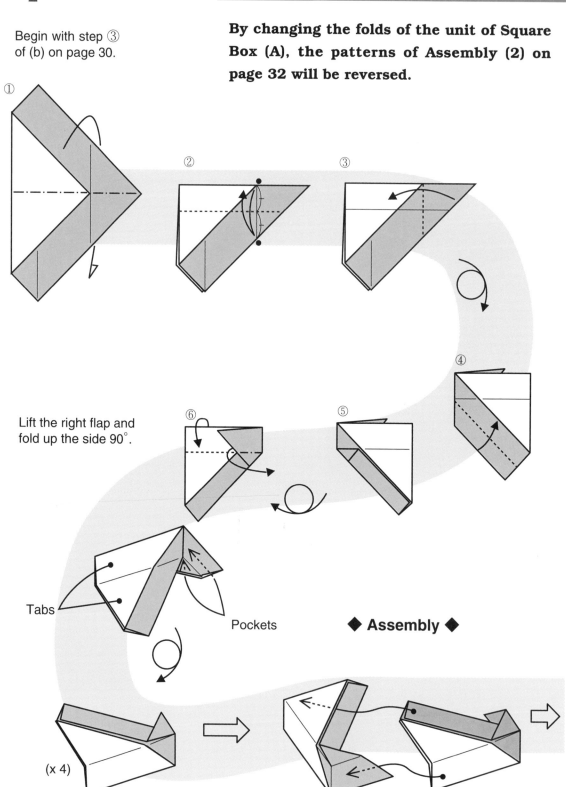

Lift the right flap and fold up the side 90°.

Tabs

Pockets

◆ **Assembly** ◆

(x 4)

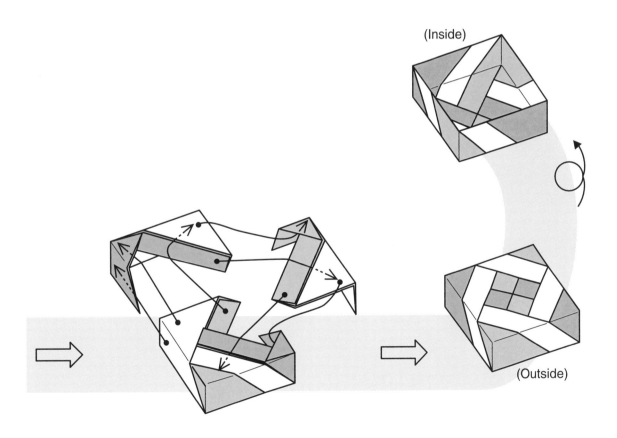

(Inside)

(Outside)

Square Box C

A box with small ornaments on top.

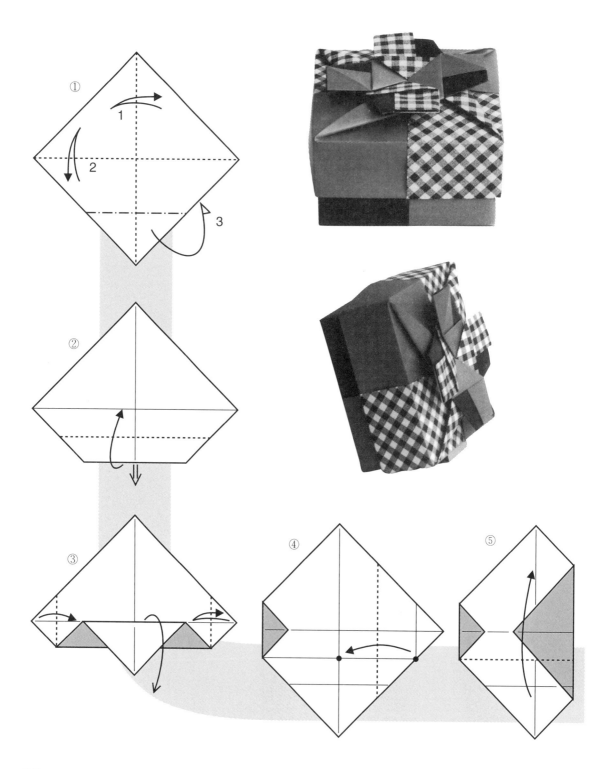

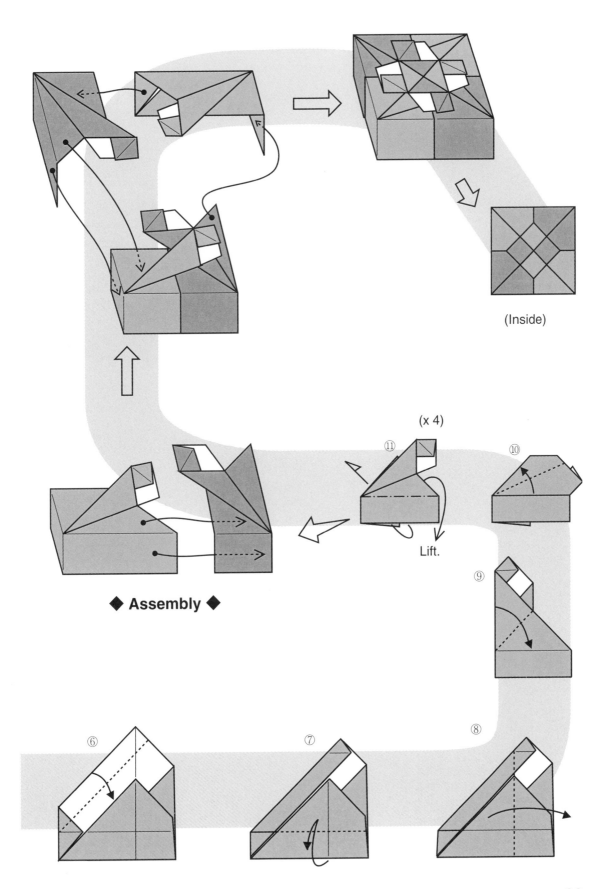

(Inside)

(x 4)

⑪

⑩

Lift.

⑨

◆ **Assembly** ◆

⑥

⑦

⑧

39

Square Box *D*

A box with a knob.

Begin with step ⑪
on page 39.

① Unfold.
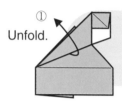

②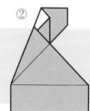

③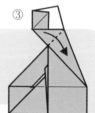

④
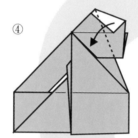

⑤
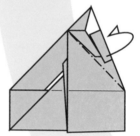

Unfold and
fold up the side 90°.

⑥
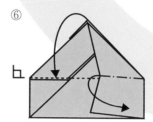

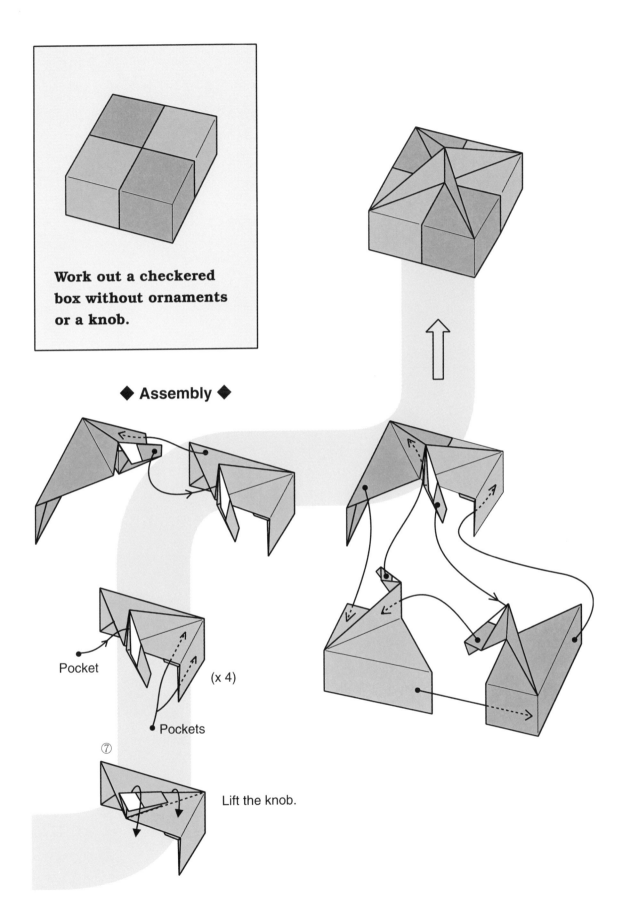

Work out a checkered box without ornaments or a knob.

◆ **Assembly** ◆

Pocket

Pockets

(x 4)

⑦

Lift the knob.

Body of Square Box 1

The most simple fold and assembly.
The partition is very useful.

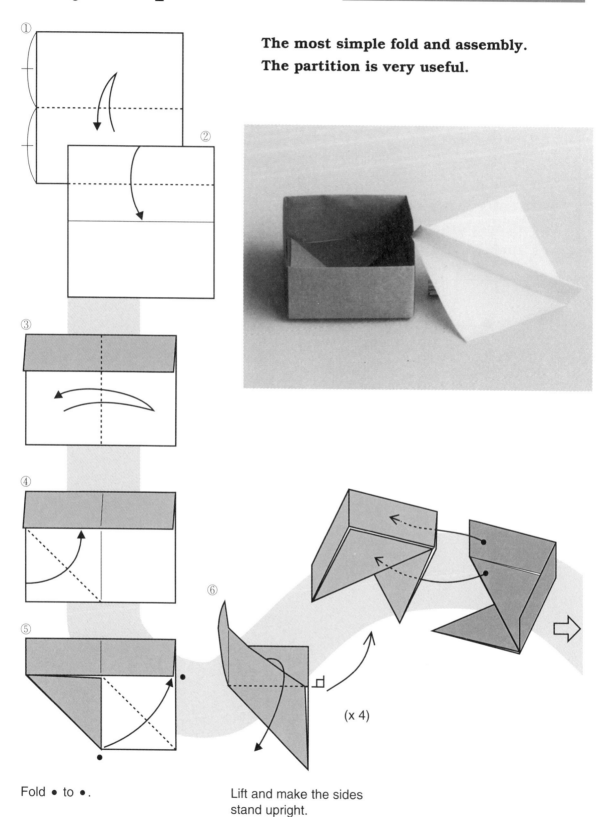

Fold • to •.

Lift and make the sides
stand upright.

(x 4)

Partition 1

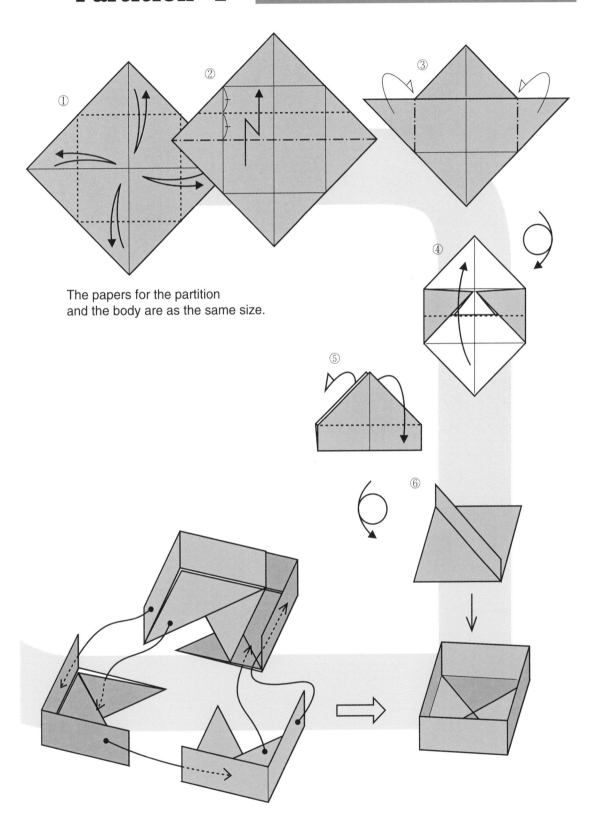

The papers for the partition
and the body are as the same size.

Body of Square Box 2

Once the box is assembled and locked, it will be very firm and solid.

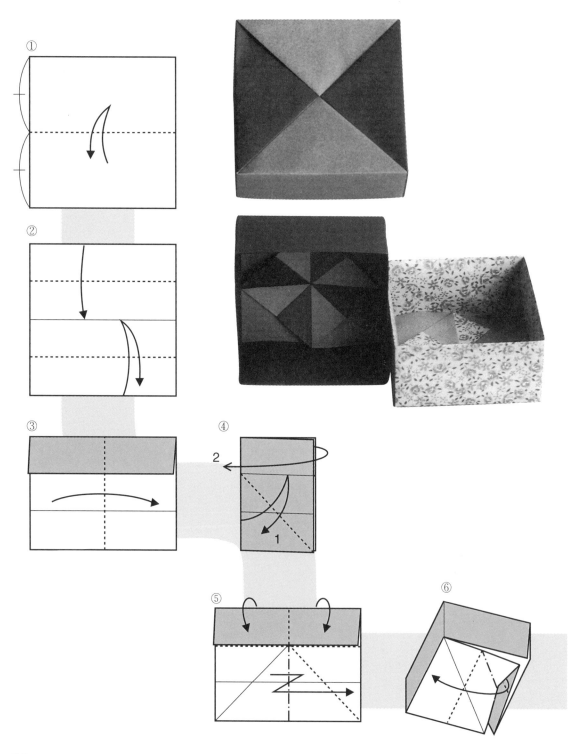

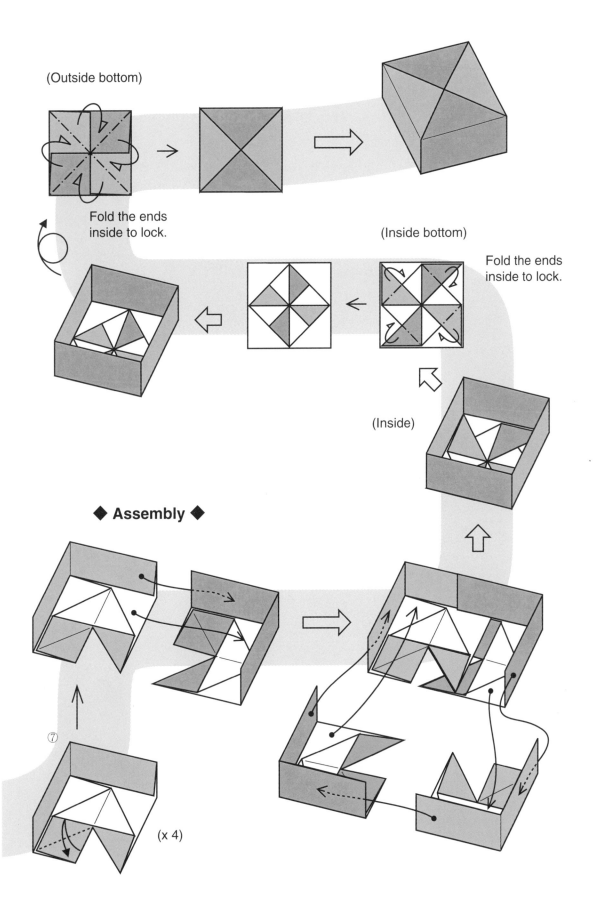

(Outside bottom)

Fold the ends
inside to lock.

(Inside bottom)

Fold the ends
inside to lock.

(Inside)

◆ **Assembly** ◆

⑦

(x 4)

Body of Square Box 3

This box is paired with Square Boxes C and D.

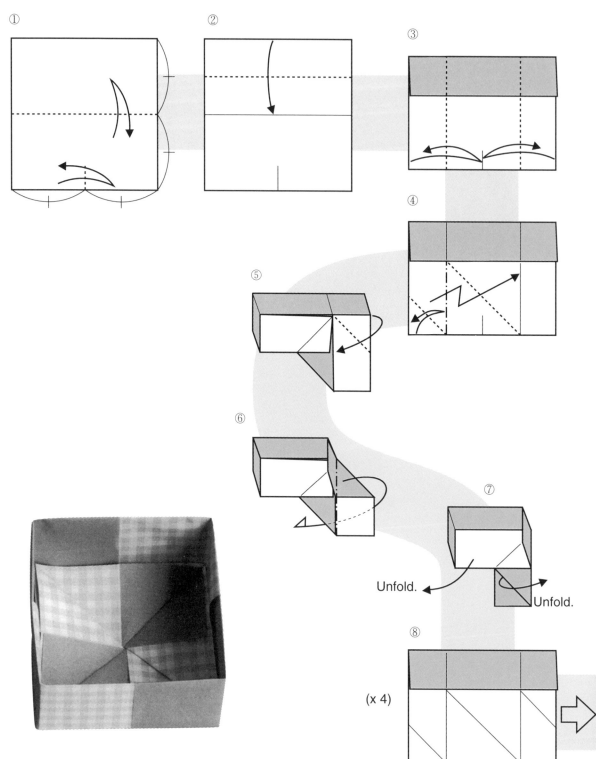

① ② ③ ④ ⑤ ⑥

⑦ Unfold. Unfold.

⑧ (x 4)

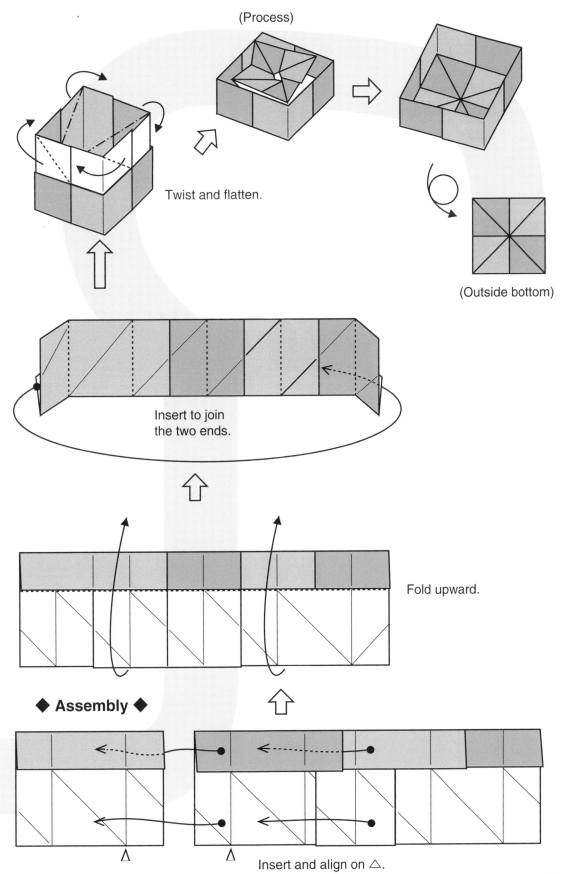

(Process)

Twist and flatten.

(Outside bottom)

Insert to join
the two ends.

Fold upward.

◆ **Assembly** ◆

Insert and align on △.

47

Body of Square Box *E*

The small plates on page 54 will fit into this box.
By changing the length of L in step ④,
you can make nesting boxes.

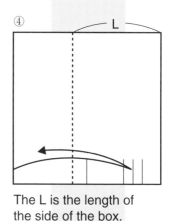

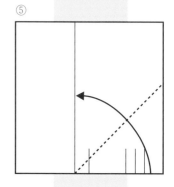

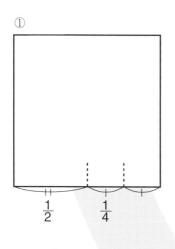

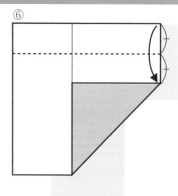

The L is the length of
the side of the box.

①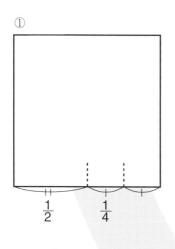

$\frac{1}{2}$ $\frac{1}{4}$

②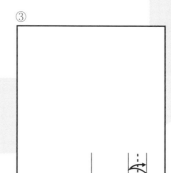

③

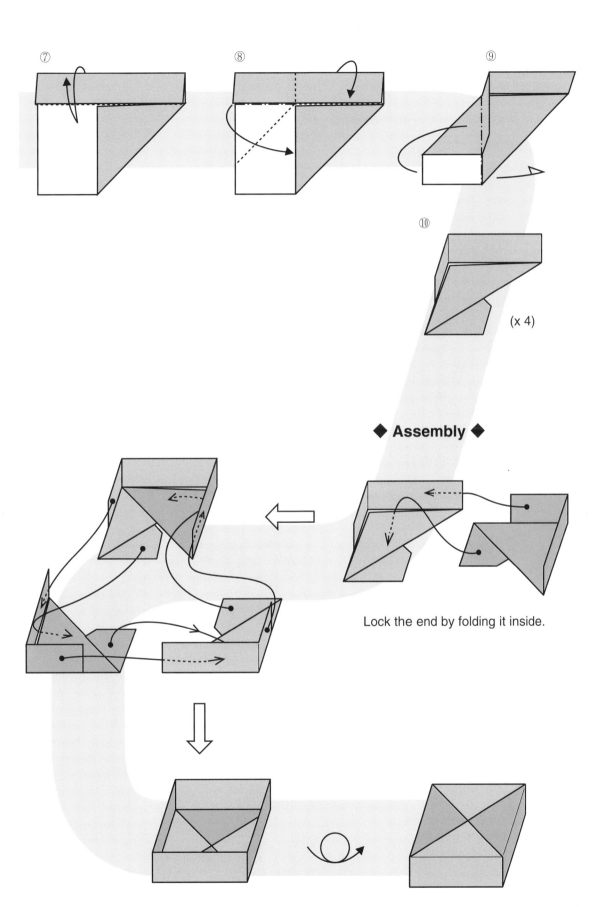

⑦ ⑧ ⑨

⑩

(x 4)

◆ **Assembly** ◆

Lock the end by folding it inside.

Variation of Square Box E

─ E′ ─

Begin with step ⑦ on page 49.

①
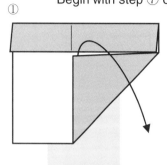

②
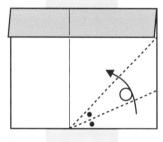

③
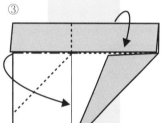

④
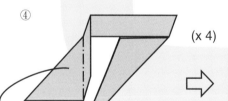

(× 4)

◆ Assembly ◆

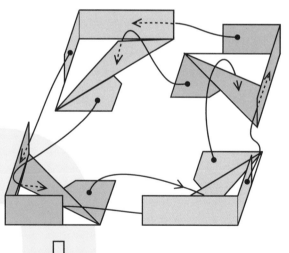

It is possible to assemble by mixing this unit with the units of Box (E) on page 49.

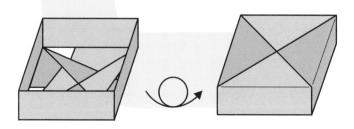

— E″ —

Begin with step ⑦ on page 49.

①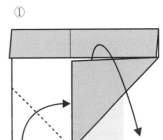

②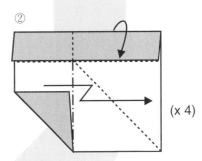

(x 4)

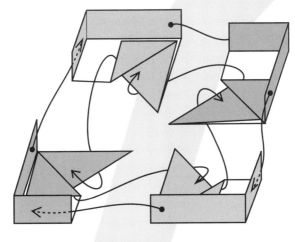

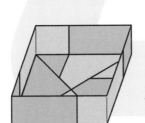 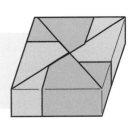

Lid of Square Box *E*

The L is the length of the side of the box.
If you fold as in the drawing, you can get the lid of the box.
If you change the length of L, you can get nesting boxes.

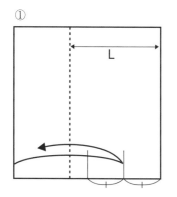

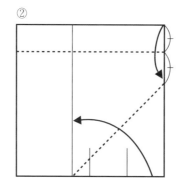

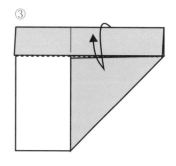

The folding and assembly
are the same as those
shown on pages 49-51.

Partition 2

If you open the center pocket, you can put something into it.
It is also possible to fold the partition on page 43 like this one.

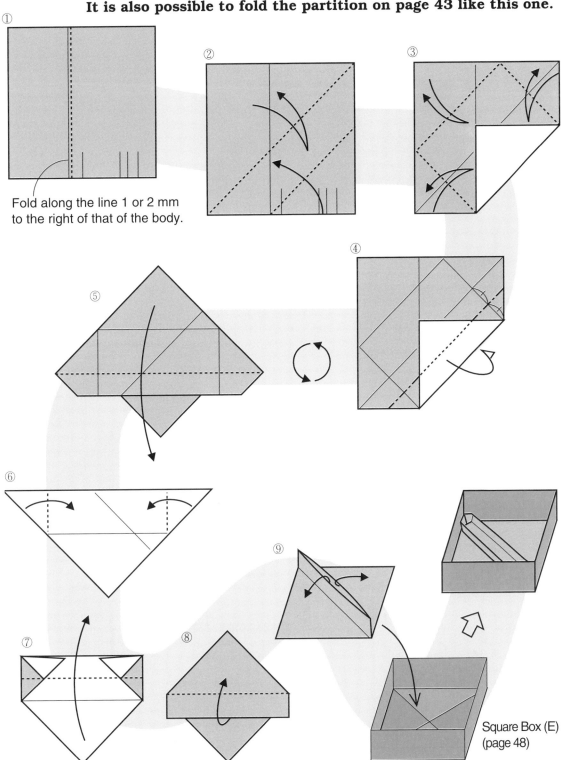

Fold along the line 1 or 2 mm
to the right of that of the body.

Square Box (E)
(page 48)

Small Plate

You can put these plates into the Square Box
on page 48 or use them individually.

① ② ③ ④ ⑤

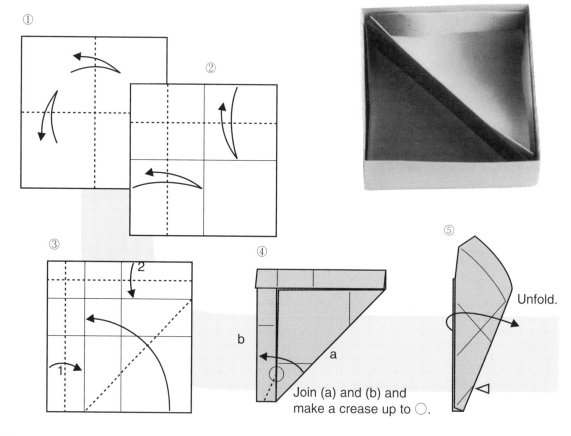

b

a

Join (a) and (b) and
make a crease up to ○.

Unfold.

1

2

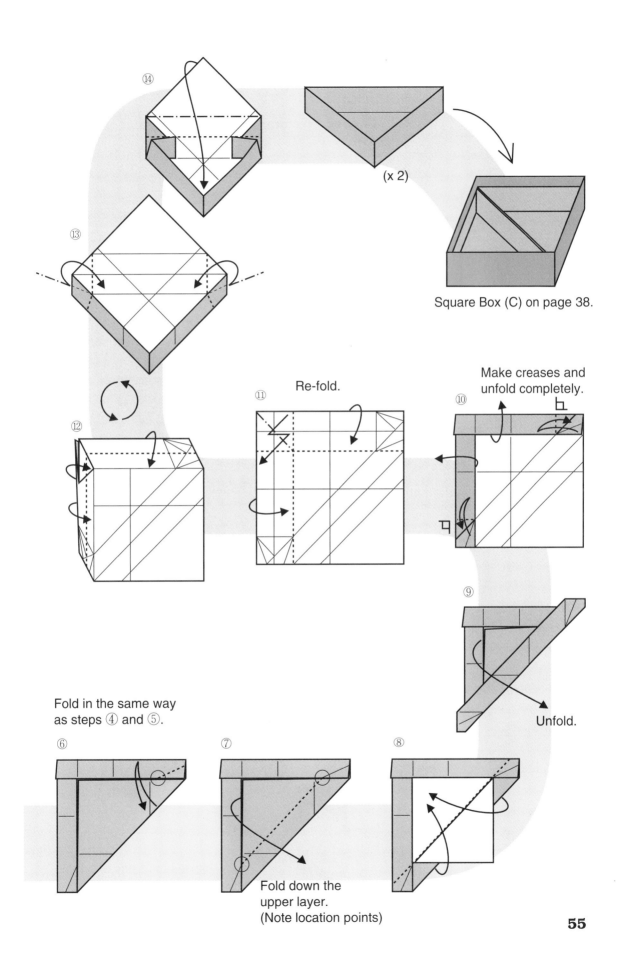

⑭

(x 2)

Square Box (C) on page 38.

⑬

⑫

⑪ Re-fold.

⑩ Make creases and unfold completely.

⑨ Unfold.

Fold in the same way as steps ④ and ⑤.

⑥

⑦

⑧

Fold down the upper layer. (Note location points)

Square Box *F*

A deep box made from rectangular papers.

Rectangular paper

①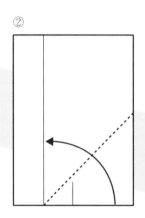

②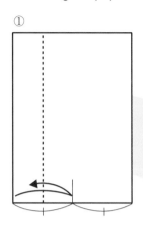

③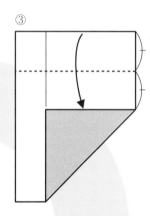

④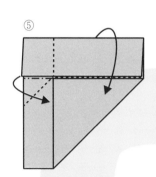

⑤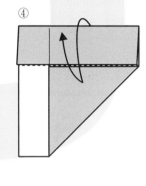

⑥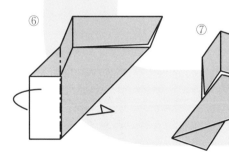

⑦ (x 4)

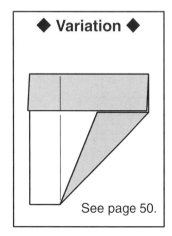

◆ **Variation** ◆

See page 50.

Make 4 units and assemble
as shown on page 49.

56

Nesting Square Boxes *F*

If you change the length in step ① on the
left page, you can make nesting boxes.
The L is the length of the side of the box.

Large

L

Small

Flowery Plate

A container which looks like an open flower.

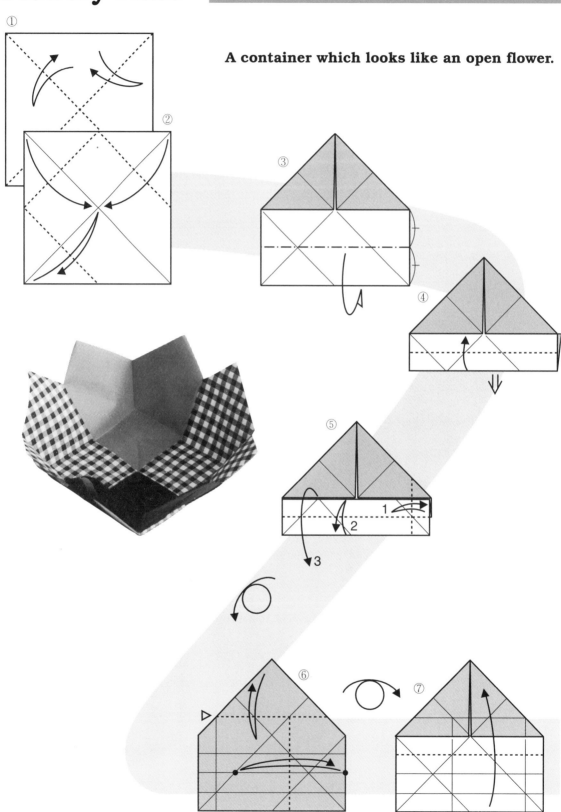

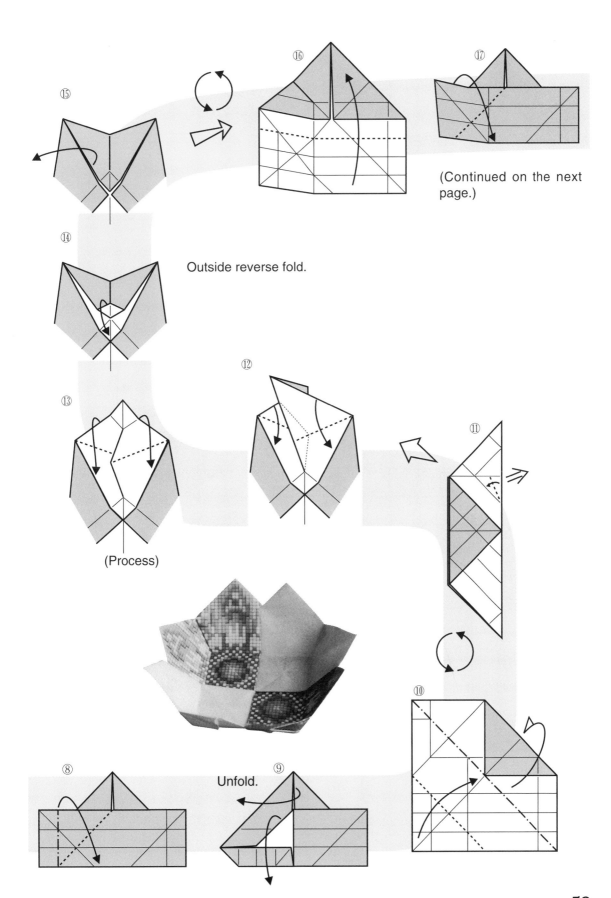

⑯

⑰

(Continued on the next page.)

⑮

⑭

Outside reverse fold.

⑬

⑫

⑪

(Process)

⑩

⑧

⑨

Unfold.

59

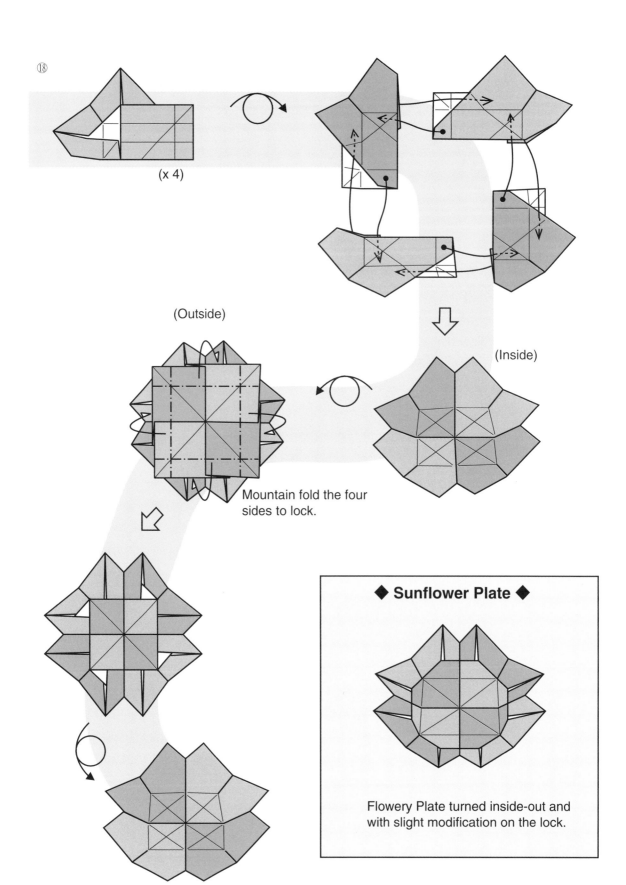

⑱

(x 4)

(Outside)

(Inside)

Mountain fold the four sides to lock.

◆ **Sunflower Plate** ◆

Flowery Plate turned inside-out and with slight modification on the lock.

60

Heart-shaped Flowery Plate

A plate surrounded by four hearts.

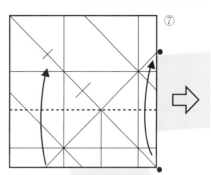

⑦

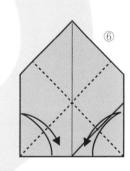

⑤

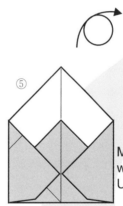

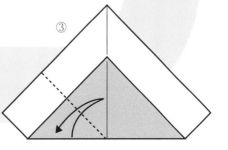

⑥

Make creases together
with the under layers.
Unfold completely.

①

$\frac{1}{4}$

④

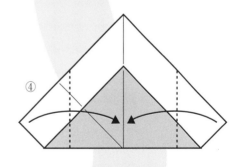

②

③

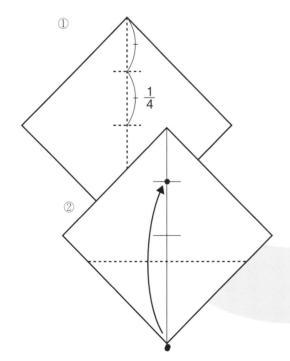

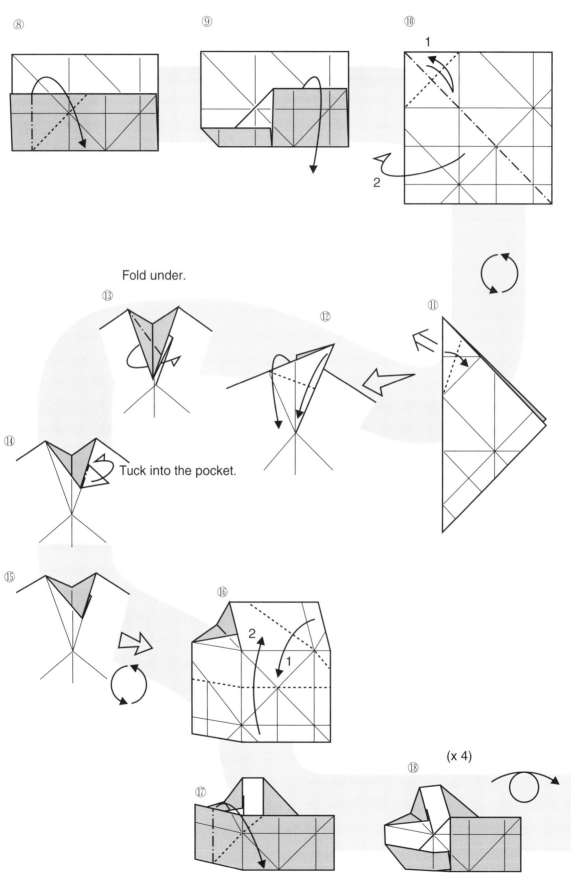

Fold under.

Tuck into the pocket.

(x 4)

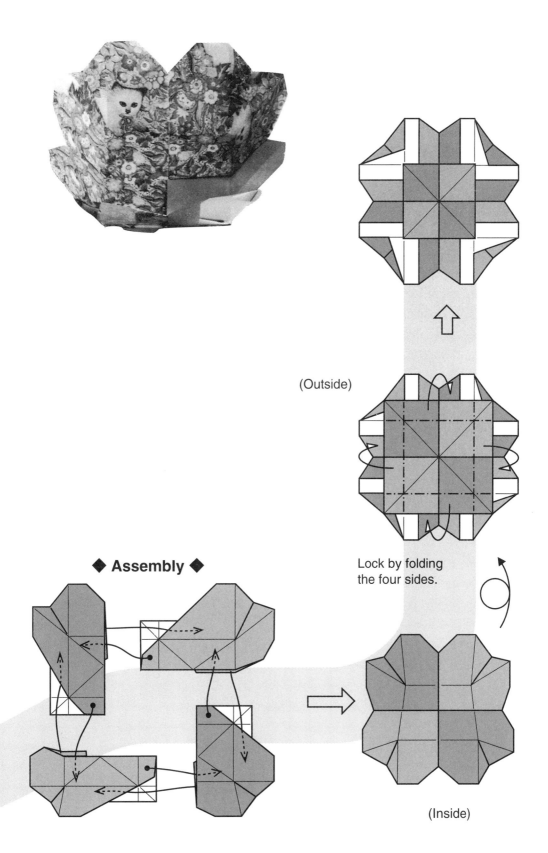

(Outside)

Lock by folding
the four sides.

◆ **Assembly** ◆

(Inside)

Octagon Box - *Flowery Pinwheel*

This is one of my favorite box.

You need 16 pieces of paper, 8 for the body and 8 for the lid.

A lot of work is required to fold all the units, but you will certainly be satisfied with the result — the gorgeous volume and the beauty in symmetry.

By changing the assembly, you will get different patterns.

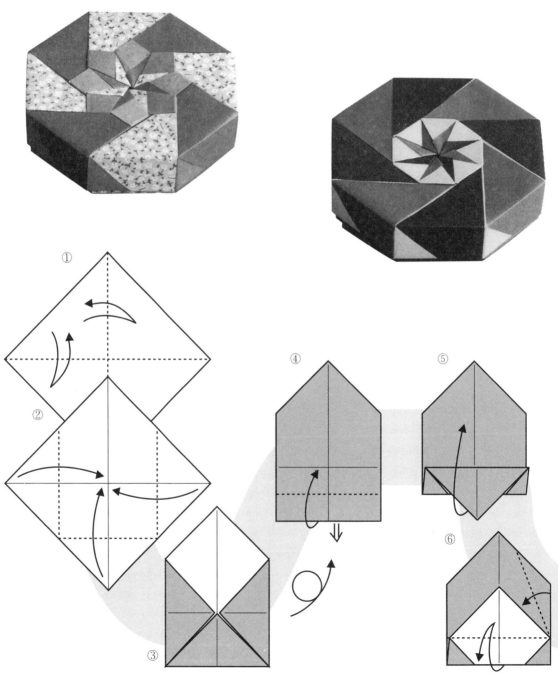

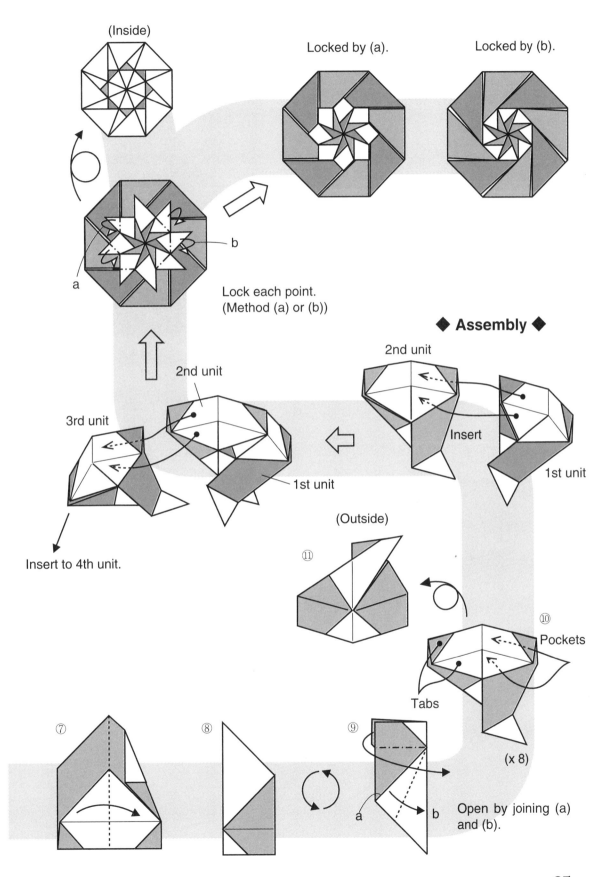

(Inside)

Locked by (a).

Locked by (b).

a

b

Lock each point.
(Method (a) or (b))

◆ **Assembly** ◆

2nd unit

2nd unit

3rd unit

Insert

1st unit

1st unit

Insert to 4th unit.

(Outside)

⑪

⑩

Pockets

Tabs

(x 8)

⑦

⑧

⑨

a

b

Open by joining (a)
and (b).

65

Octagon Box - *Starry Pinwheel*

Change the tabs and pockets of 'Flowery Pinwheel' and reverse the direction of insertion.

Begin with step ⑩ on page 65.

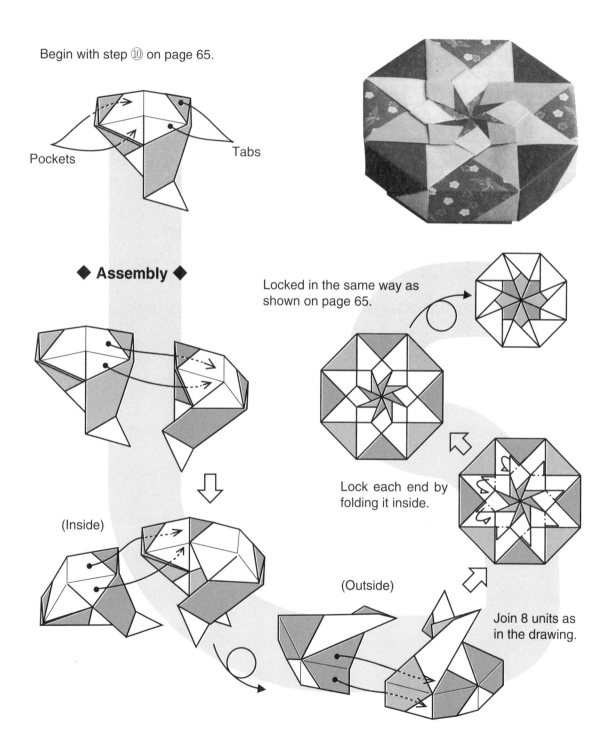

Pockets

Tabs

◆ **Assembly** ◆

Locked in the same way as shown on page 65.

Lock each end by folding it inside.

(Inside)

(Outside)

Join 8 units as in the drawing.

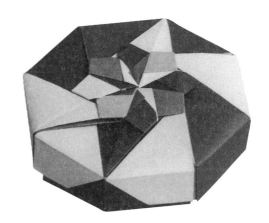

◆ Mixed Assembly ◆

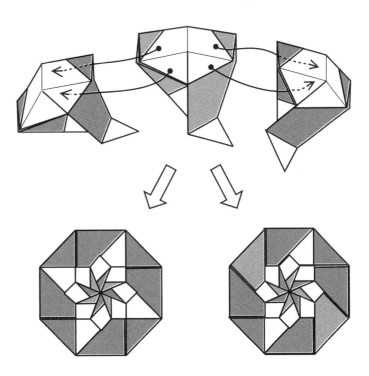

Octagon Box - *Pinwheel*

Begin with step ⑦ on page 65.

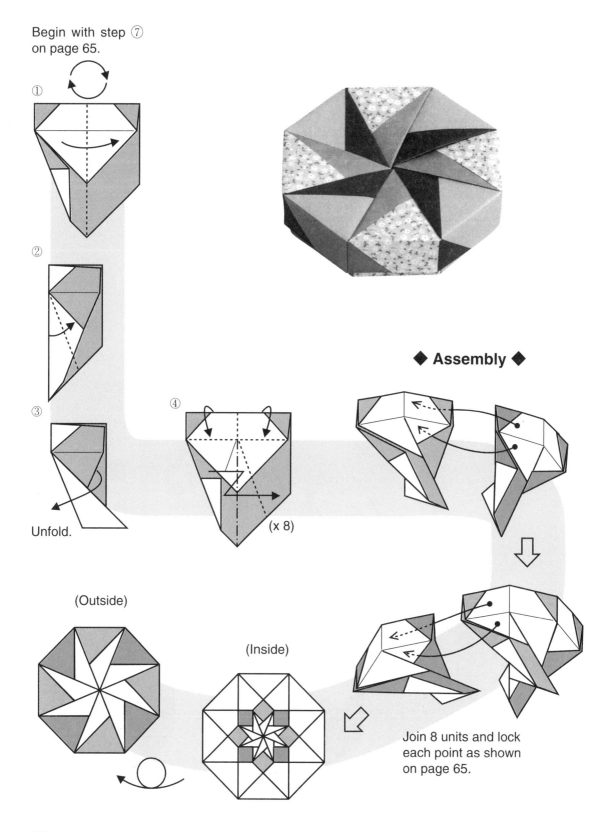

①

②

③

Unfold.

④

(x 8)

◆ **Assembly** ◆

(Outside)

(Inside)

Join 8 units and lock each point as shown on page 65.

Octagon Box - *Plain*

Plain units without patterns. You can also join them with different units.

Begin with step ③ on page 64.

①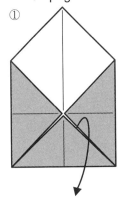

②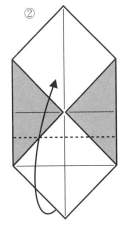

③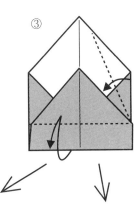

a (Flowery Pinwheel Type)   b (Pinwheel Type)

Continue with steps ⑦ to ⑪ on page 65.

Continue with steps ① to ④ on page 68.

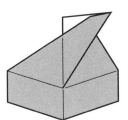   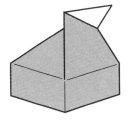

Octagon Box - *Double Pinwheel*

Begin with step ⑥
on page 64.

**By changing the assembly, you can get
different patterns.**

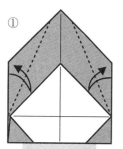

①

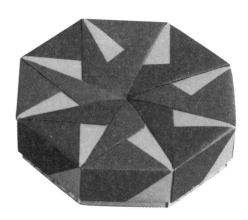

②

③

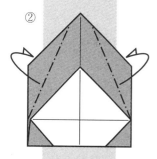

④

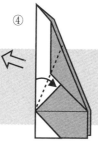

Pull out the
under layer.

⑤

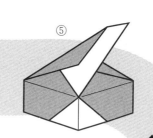

(x 8)

◆ **Assembly 1** ◆

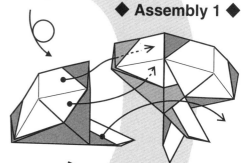

Join 8 units as
shown.

(Inside)

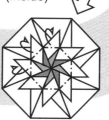

Lock each end by
folding it inside.

(Outside)

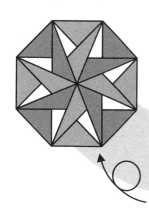

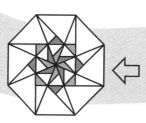

◆ Assembly 2 ◆

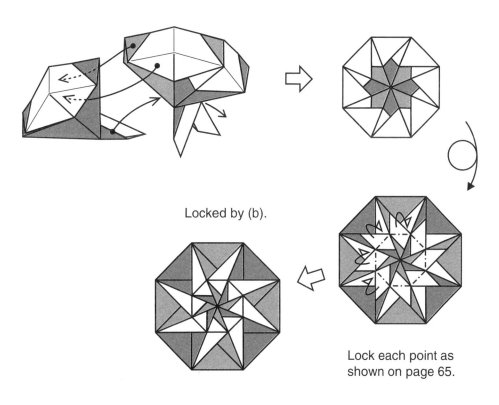

Locked by (b).

Lock each point as
shown on page 65.

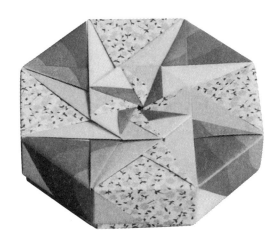

Variation of Octagon Box

Make different variations by making the most of the front and back of the paper. You may mix different units to produce a variety of patterns.

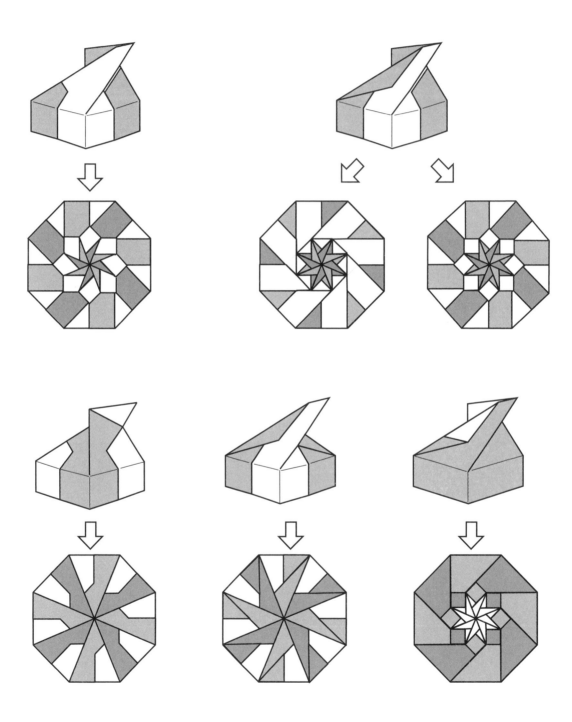

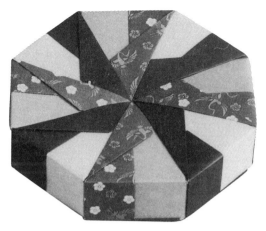

Octagon Box variation (p.72)

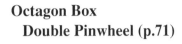

Octagon Box
Double Pinwheel (p.71)

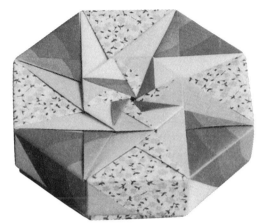

Octagon Box variation (p.72)

Octagon Box variation (p.72)

Heptagon Box
Flowery Pinwheel (p.79)

Body of Octagon Box

The L of ②′ is the length of the side of the box.
Use ③′ as a template for the measurement of the other paper.
After you have finished the body, work out and try to fold the lid.

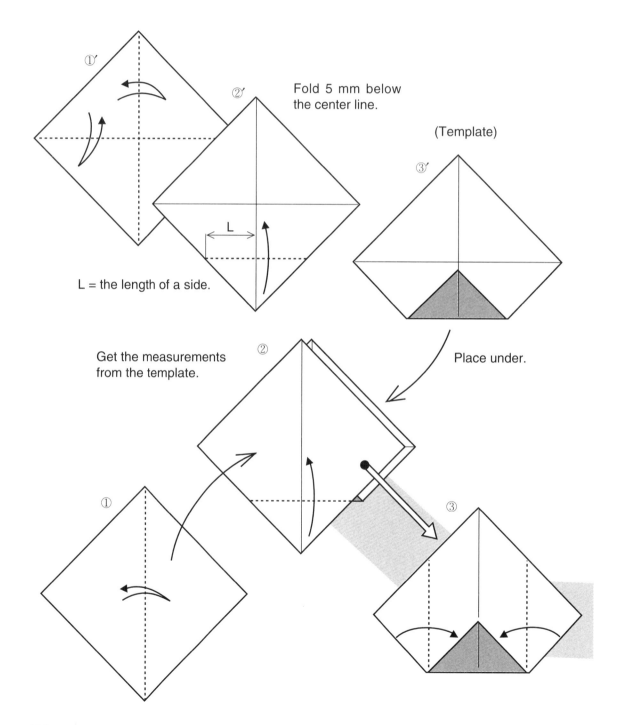

①′

②′ Fold 5 mm below the center line.

L

L = the length of a side.

(Template)

③′

Get the measurements from the template.

②

Place under.

①

③

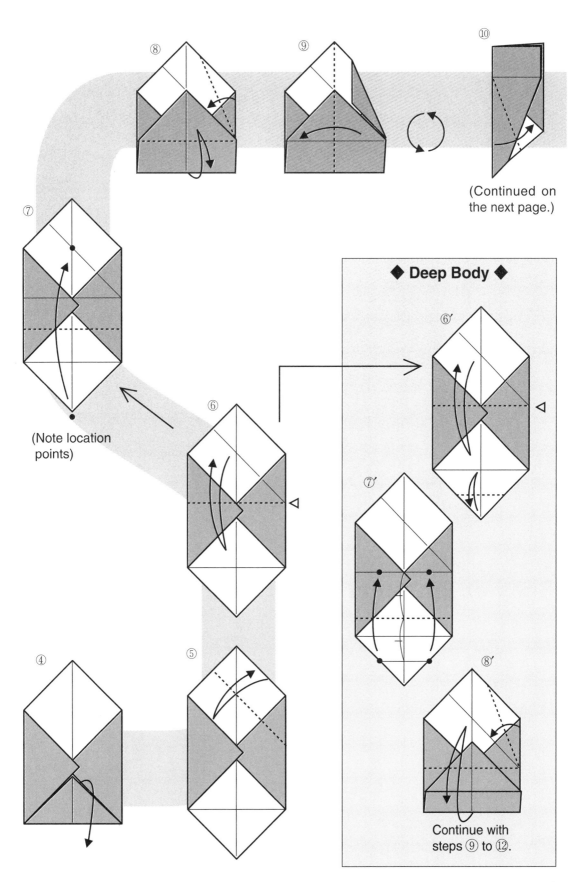

⑧ ⑨ ⑩

(Continued on the next page.)

⑦

(Note location points)

◆ **Deep Body** ◆

⑥′

⑦′

⑥

④ ⑤

⑧′

Continue with steps ⑨ to ⑫.

75

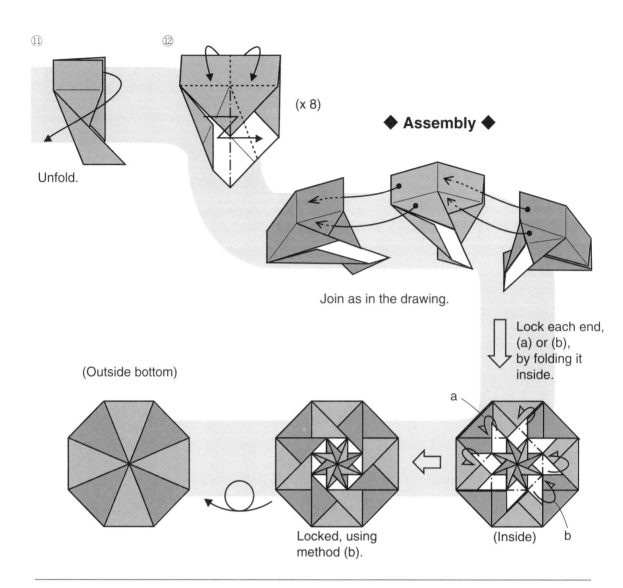

⑪

Unfold.

⑫

(x 8)

◆ **Assembly** ◆

Join as in the drawing.

Lock each end,
(a) or (b),
by folding it
inside.

a

(Outside bottom)

Locked, using
method (b).

(Inside)

b

Body of Pinwheel Pattern

Begin with step ⑦ on page 75.

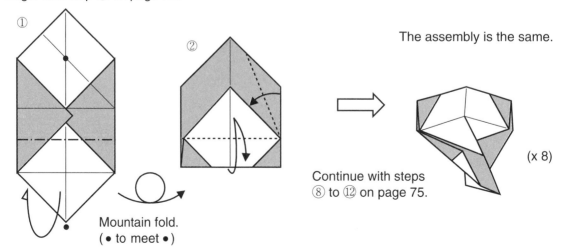

①

②

The assembly is the same.

(x 8)

Continue with steps
⑧ to ⑫ on page 75.

Mountain fold.
(• to meet •)

Nesting Octagon Boxes

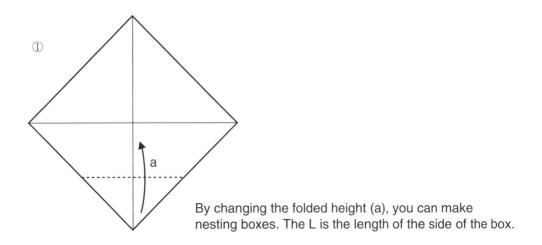

①

By changing the folded height (a), you can make nesting boxes. The L is the length of the side of the box.

(Large shallow box)   (Small deep box)

L   L

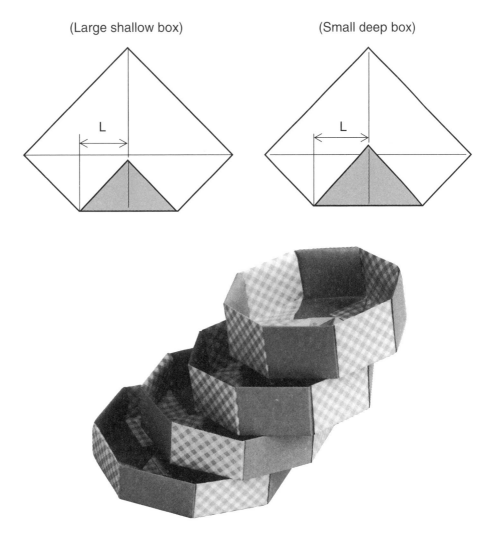

Heptagon Box - *Flowery Pinwheel*

**It is difficult to fold at exact angles by this method,
but the margin of error is slight.
With repeated folding and joining, the error will be minimized
and will not affect the whole shape.**

Begin with step ⑥
on page 64.

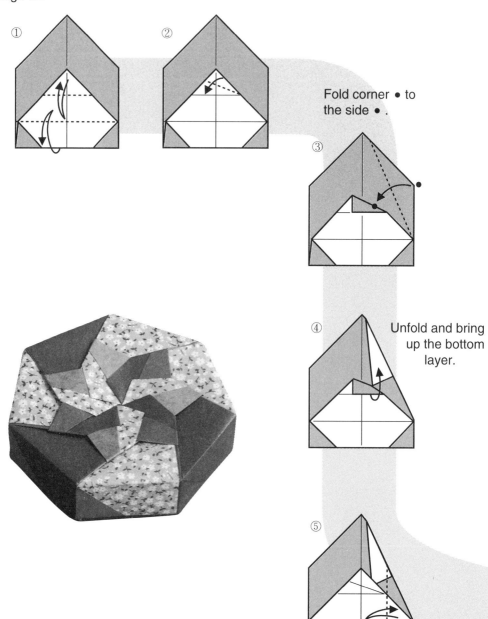

① ②

Fold corner • to
the side • .

③

④ Unfold and bring
up the bottom
layer.

⑤

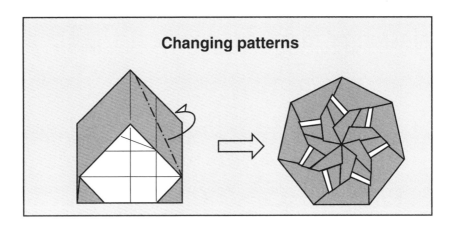

Changing patterns

(Inside)　　　　　　　(Outside)

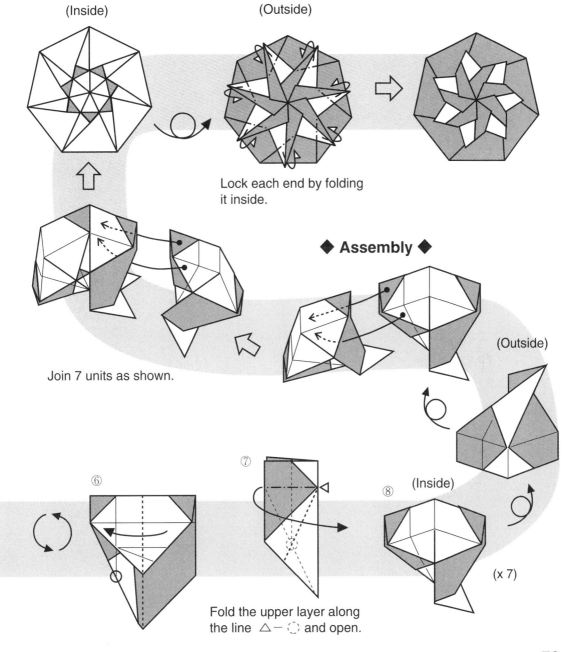

Lock each end by folding
it inside.

◆ **Assembly** ◆

(Outside)

Join 7 units as shown.

(Inside)

(x 7)

⑥　　　　⑦

Fold the upper layer along
the line △ — ⟳ and open.

Variation of Flowery Pinwheel

A

B

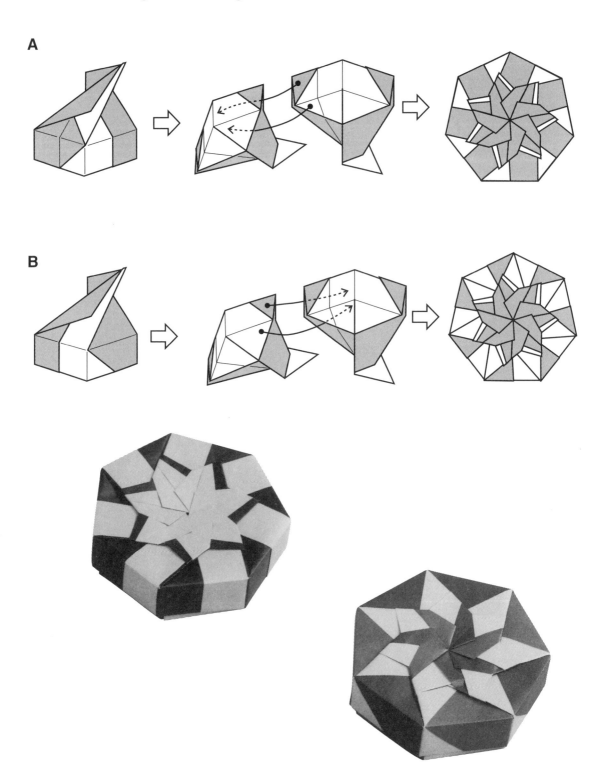

Heptagon Box - *Starry Pinwheel*

Begin with step ⑥
on page 79.

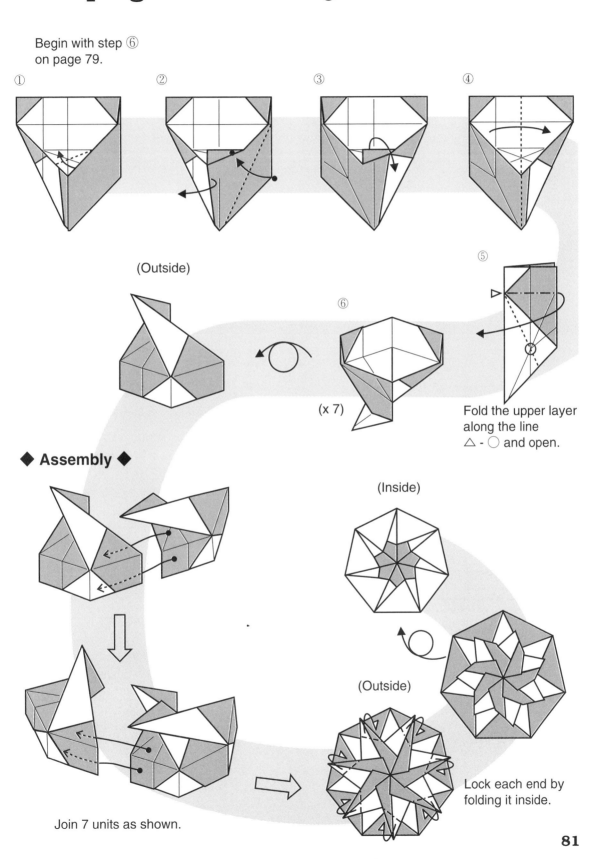

① ② ③ ④

⑤

Fold the upper layer
along the line
△ - ○ and open.

(Outside)

⑥

(x 7)

◆ **Assembly** ◆

(Inside)

(Outside)

Join 7 units as shown.

Lock each end by
folding it inside.

Heptagon Box - *Pinwheel*

Begin with step ⑧
on page 79.

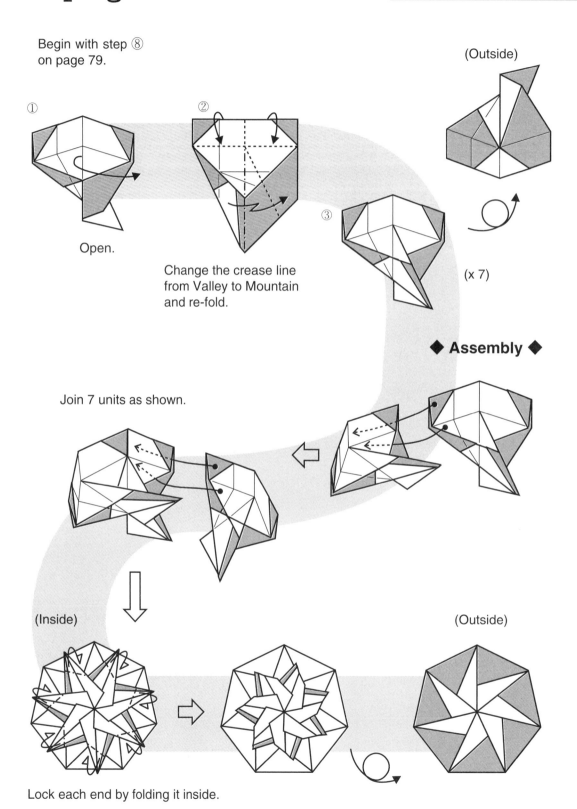

(Outside)

①

Open.

②

Change the crease line
from Valley to Mountain
and re-fold.

③

(x 7)

◆ **Assembly** ◆

Join 7 units as shown.

(Inside)

(Outside)

Lock each end by folding it inside.

Heptagon Box - *Plain*

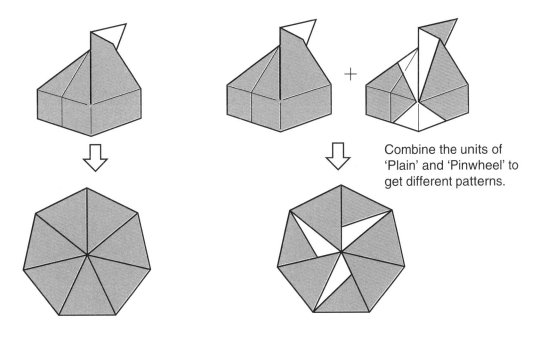

Combine the units of 'Plain' and 'Pinwheel' to get different patterns.

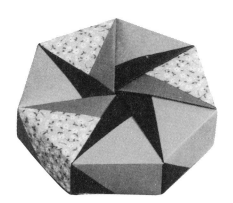

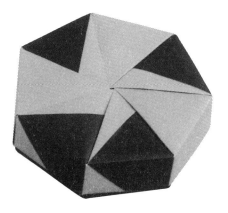

Heptagon Box - *Double Pinwheel*

Begin with step ⑥
on page 81.

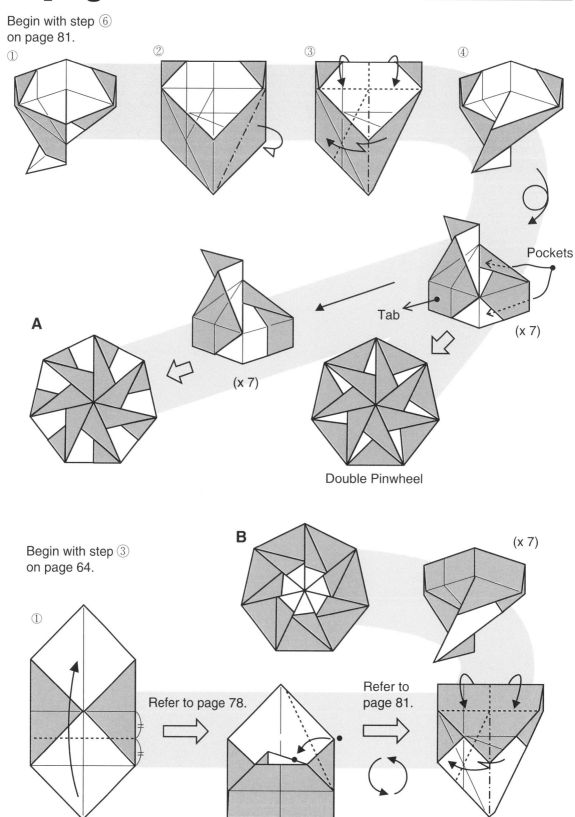

① ② ③ ④

Pockets

Tab

(x 7)

A

(x 7)

Double Pinwheel

Begin with step ③
on page 64.

B

(x 7)

①

Refer to page 78.

Refer to
page 81.

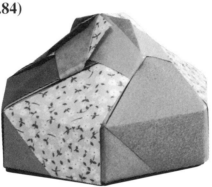

Heptagon Box
Double Pinwheel (A) (p.84)

Heptagon Box
Double Pinwheel (B) (p.84)

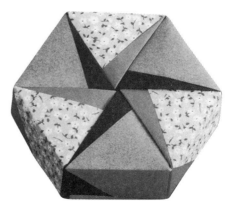

Hexagon Box
Steeple-Crowned Cap (p.94)

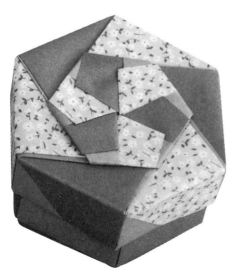

Hexagon Box
Flowery Pinwheel (p.89)

Hexagon Box
Pinwheel (p.90)

Body of Heptagon Box

Begin with step ⑥ on page 75.

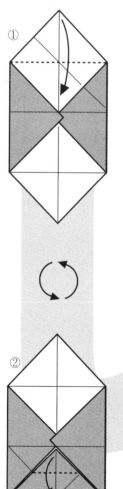

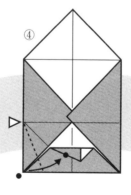

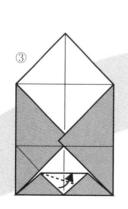

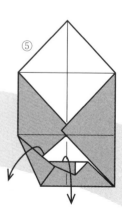

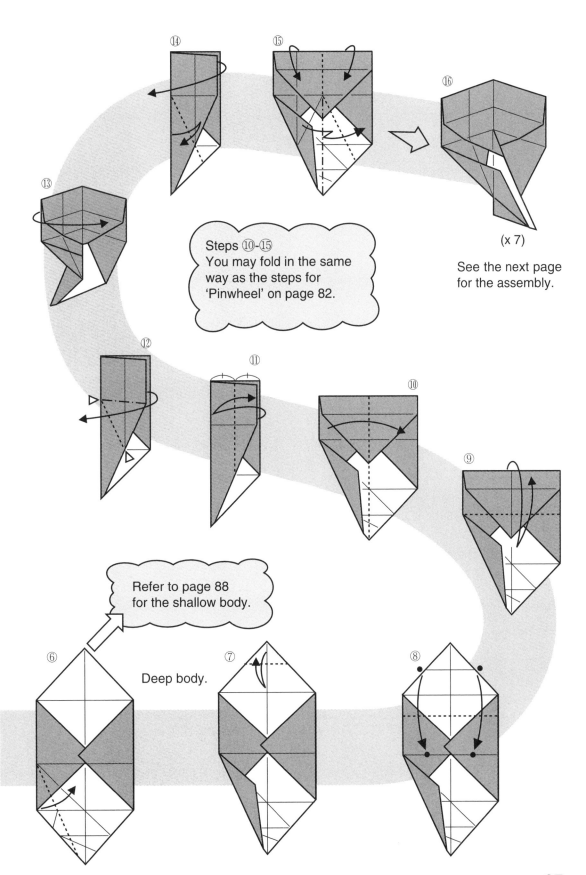

⑭

⑮

⑯

(x 7)

See the next page
for the assembly.

⑬

Steps ⑩-⑮
You may fold in the same
way as the steps for
'Pinwheel' on page 82.

⑫

⑪

⑩

⑨

Refer to page 88
for the shallow body.

⑥

⑦

Deep body.

⑧

◆ Assembly ◆

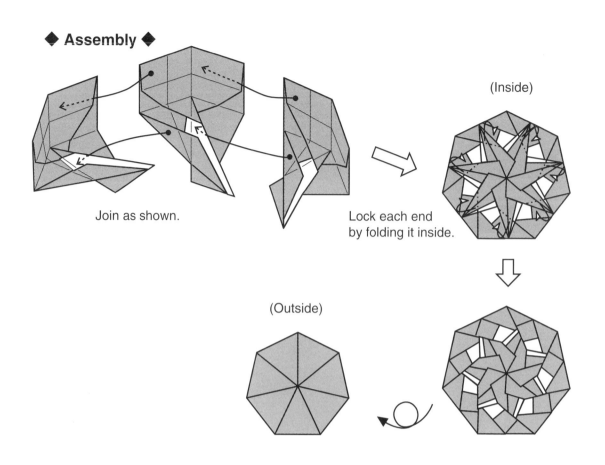

Join as shown.

Lock each end
by folding it inside.

(Inside)

(Outside)

Shallow Body

Begin with step ⑥
on page 75.

Continue with
steps ⑩ to ⑯
on page 87.

① ② ③ ④ ⑤

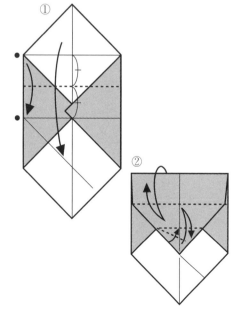
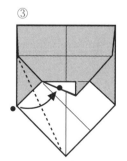
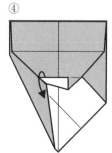
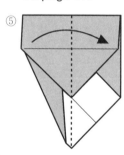
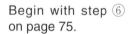

Hexagon Box - *Flowery Pinwheel*

The basic fold is the same as that of the Octagon and Heptagon Boxes. The angle of the Hexagon Box is derived in step ②.

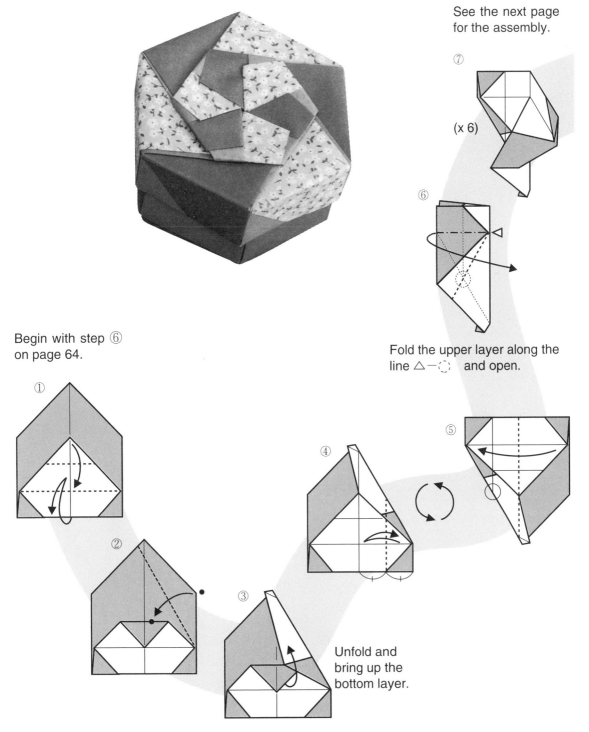

See the next page for the assembly.

⑦

(x 6)

⑥

Fold the upper layer along the line △—◌ and open.

Begin with step ⑥ on page 64.

①

②

③

④

⑤

Unfold and bring up the bottom layer.

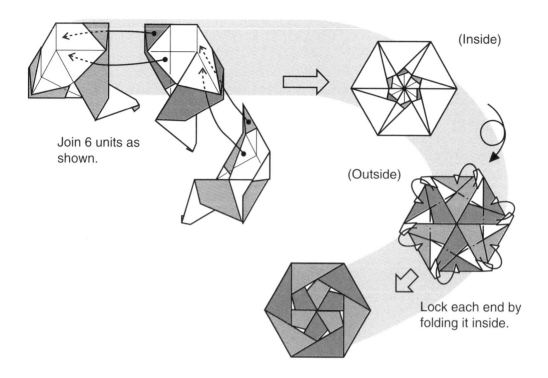

Join 6 units as shown.

(Inside)

(Outside)

Lock each end by folding it inside.

Hexagon Box - *Pinwheel*

Begin with step ⑦ on page 89.

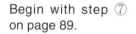

①

②

Open.

Change the crease line from Valley to Mountain and re-fold.

(x 6)

(Outside)

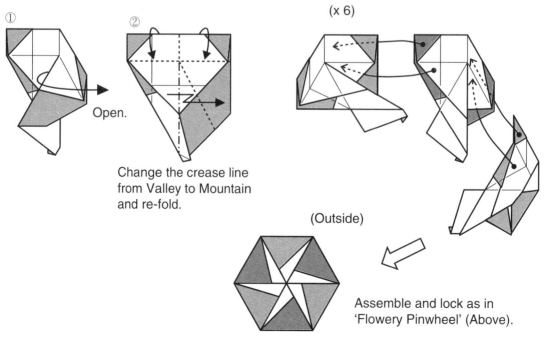

Assemble and lock as in 'Flowery Pinwheel' (Above).

Hexagon Box - *Starry Pinwheel*

Begin with step ⑦
on page 89.

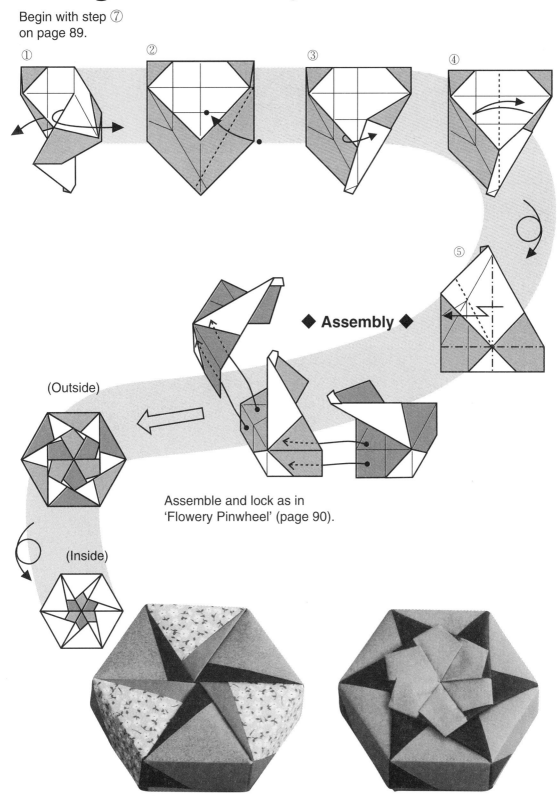

◆ **Assembly** ◆

(Outside)

Assemble and lock as in
'Flowery Pinwheel' (page 90).

(Inside)

Body of Hexagon Box

Begin with step ⑧
on page 75.

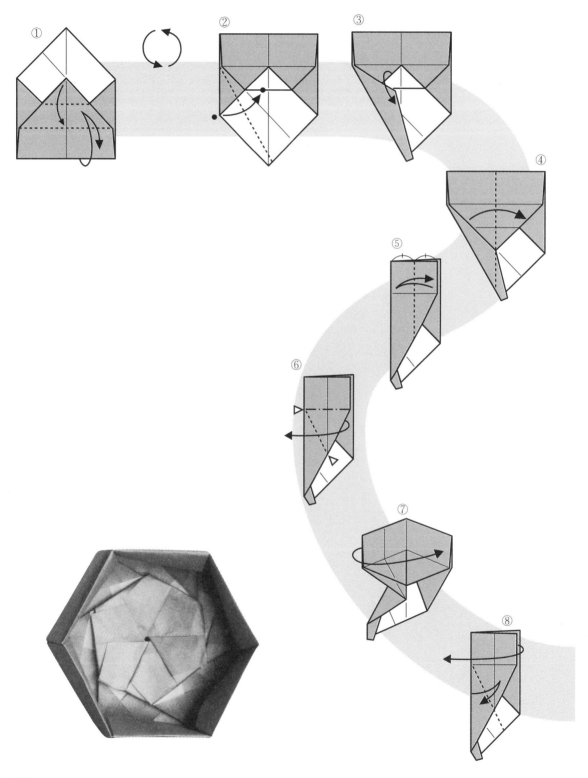

Deep Body

Begin with step ④
on page 75.

Continue with
steps ④ - ⑨
on the left page.

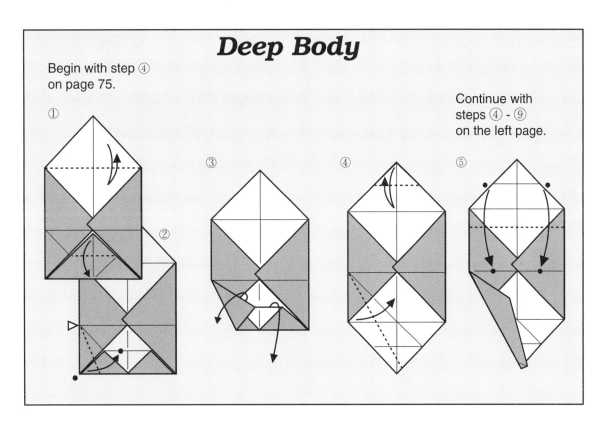

(Outside)

(Inside)

When 6 units have been joined,
lock each point as shown on
page 90.

Steps ④ - ⑨ may be
folded the same way as
'Pinwheel' on page 90.

◆ **Assembly** ◆

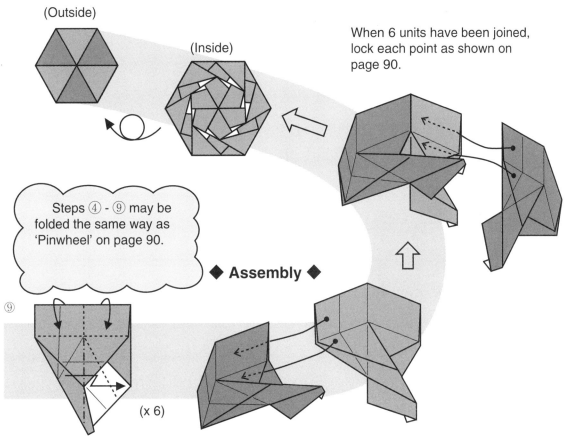

(x 6)

Hexagon Box - *Steeple-crowned Cap*

If you join 6 units of the Octagon Box, you can make
the Steeple-crowned lid of the Hexagon Box.
Try out other variations with 'Flowery Pinwheel,'
'Starry Pinwheel,' and 'Mixed Assembly.'

A

From step ⑪ on page 65.

①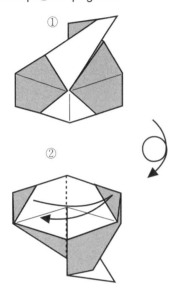

②

B

From step ④ on page 68.

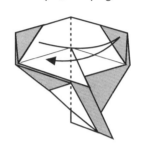

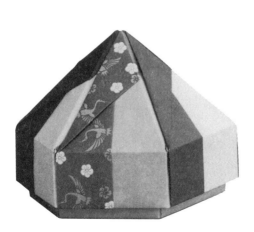

How to fold
Hexagon, Heptagon and Octagon Boxes

The drawings below show how the different angles are derived from the 'Pinwheel.' You will get much folding pleasure by folding a set of three different boxes.

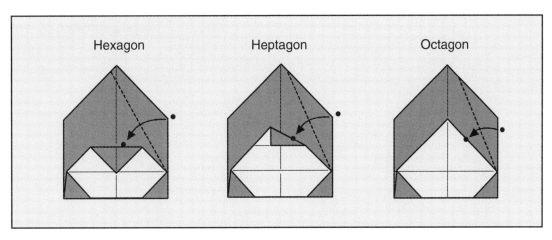

Hexagon Heptagon Octagon

ORIGAMI BOOKS
from Japan Publications

BRILLIANT ORIGAMI: A Collection of Original Designs by David Brill
240 pp., 7 1/4 x 10 1/4 in., 8 pp. color, 215 pp. line drawings, paperback.
ISBN: 0-87040-896-8

COMPLETE ORIGAMI COLLECTION, THE, by Toshie Takahama
160 pp., 7 1/4 x 10 1/4 in., 8 pp. color, 147 pp. line drawings, paperback.
ISBN: 0-87040-960-3

CREATIVE ORIGAMI by Kunihiko Kasahara
180 pp., 8 1/4 x 11 3/4 in., 8 pp. b/w photos, 160 pp. line drawings, paperback.
ISBN: 0-87040-411-3

FLYING BIRD ORIGAMI by Yoshihiko Momotani
70 pp., 7 1/4 x 9 in., 4 pp. color, 62 pp. line drawings, paperback.
ISBN: 0-87040-908-5

HAPPY ORIGAMI: Simple & Easy Origami for Families by Toshie Takahama
Boxed set, board-book: 30 pp., 6 x 6 in., 30 pp. full color, plus origami paper: 6 x 6 in., 70 sheets.
ISBN: 0-87040-986-7

JOY OF ORIGAMI, THE, by Toshie Takahama
104 pp., 7 1/4 x 10 1/4 in., 8 pp. color, 61 pp. line drawings, paperback.
ISBN: 0-87040-603-5

KUSUDAMA: Ball Origami by Makoto Yamaguchi
72 pp., 7 1/4 x 10 1/4 in., 8 pp. color, 65 pp. line drawings, paperback.
ISBN: 0-87040-863-1

MAGIC OF ORIGAMI, THE, by Alice Gray and Kunihiko Kasahara with cooperation of Lillian Oppenheimer and Origami Center of America
132 pp., 7 1/4 x 10 1/4 in., 122 pp. b/w photos and line drawings, paperback.
ISBN: 0-87040-624-8

ORIGAMI by Hideki Sakata
66 pp., 7 1/4 x 10 1/4 in., 66 pp. full color illustrations, paperback.
ISBN: 0-87040-580-2

ORIGAMI ANIMALS by Keiji Kitamura
88 pp., 8 1/4 x 10 1/4 in., 88 pp. full color illustrations, 12 sheets of origami paper included, paperback.
ISBN: 0-87040-941-7

ORIGAMI BOXES by Tomoko Fuse
72 pp., 7 1/4 x 10 1/4 in., 8 pp. color, 60 pp. line drawings, paperback.
ISBN: 0-87040-821-6

ORIGAMI CLASSROOM I by Dokuotei Nakano
Boxed set, board-book: 24 pp., 6 x 6 in., 24 pp. full color illustrations, plus origami paper: 6 x 6 in., 54 sheets of rainbow-color paper.
ISBN: 0-87040-912-3

ORIGAMI CLASSROOM II by Dokuotei Nakano
Boxed set, board-book: 24 pp., 6 x 6 in., 24 pp. full color illustrations, plus origami paper: 6 x 6 in., 60 sheets of rainbow-color paper.
ISBN: 0-87040-913-1

ORIGAMI HEARTS by Francis Ow Mun Yin
120 pp., 7 1/4 x 10 1/4 in., 8 pp. color, 104 pp. line drawings, paperback.
ISBN: 0-87040-957-3

ORIGAMI MADE EASY by Kunihiko Kasahara
128 pp., 6 x 8 1/4 in., 113 pp. b/w photos and line drawings, paperback.
ISBN: 0-87040-253-6

ORIGAMI OMNIBUS: Paper-folding for Everybody by Kunihiko Kasahara
384 pp., 7 1/4 x 10 1/4 in., 8 pp. color, 360 pp. line drawings, paperback.
ISBN: 0-87040-699-X

ORIGAMI TREASURE CHEST by Keiji Kitamura
80 pp., 8 1/4 x 10 1/4 in., full color, paperback.
ISBN: 0-87040-868-2

PAPER MAGIC: Pop-up Paper Craft by Masahiro Chatani
92 pp., 7 1/4 x 10 1/4 in., 16 pp. color, 72 pp. b/w photos and line drawings, paperback.
ISBN: 0-87040-757-0

POP-UP BEST GREETING CARDS by Keiko Nakazawa
122 pp., 7 1/4 x 10 1/4 in., 16 pp. color, 102 pp. b/w photos and line drawings, paperback.
ISBN: 0-87040-964-6

POP-UP GIFT CARDS by Masahiro Chatani
80 pp., 7 1/4 x 10 1/4 in., 16 pp. color, 64 pp. b/w photos and line drawings, paperback.
ISBN: 0-87040-768-6

POP-UP GEOMETRIC ORIGAMI by Masahiro Chatani and Keiko Nakazawa
86 pp., 7 1/4 x 10 1/4 in., 16 pp. color, 64 pp. b/w photos and line drawings, paperback.
ISBN: 0-87040-943-3

POP-UP ORIGAMIC ARCHITECTURE by Masahiro Chatani
88 pp., 7 1/4 x 10 1/4 in., 4 pp. color, 11 pp. b/w photos, 68 pp. line drawings, paperback.
ISBN: 0-87040-656-6

Quick & Easy ORIGAMI by Toshie Takahama
Boxed set, book: 60 pp., 6 x 4 1/8 in., 30 pp. color and 30 pp. line drawings, origami paper: 3 packs in 6 colors (90 sheets).
ISBN: 0-87040-771-6

Quick & Easy FLYING ORIGAMI by Eiji Nakamura
Boxed set, book: 60 pp., 6 x 4 1/8 in., 30 pp. color and 30 pp. line drawings, origami paper: 3 packs in 6 colors (90 sheets).
ISBN: 0-87040-925-5

Quick & Easy ORIGAMI BOXES by Tomoko Fuse
Boxed set, book: 60 pp., 6 x 4 1/8 in., 30 pp. color and 30 pp. line drawings, origami paper: 3 packs in 6 colors (90 sheets).
ISBN: 0-87040-939-5

Quick & Easy ORIGAMI CHRISTMAS by Toshie Takahama
Boxed set, book: 60 pp., 6 x 4 1/8 in., 30 pp. color and 30 pp. line drawings, origami paper: 3 packs in 6 colors (90 sheets).
ISBN: 0-87040-870-4

TRICK ORIGAMI by Yoshihide Momotani
70 pp., 7 1/4 x 9 in., 4 pp. color, 56 pp. line drawings, 12 sheets of origami paper included, paperback.
ISBN: 0-87040-929-8

UNIT ORIGAMI: Multidimensional Transformations by Tomoko Fuse
244 pp., 7 1/4 x 10 1/4 in., 8 pp. color, 220 pp. b/w photos and line drawings, paperback.
ISBN: 0-87040-852-6

WORLD OF ORIGAMI, THE, by Isao Honda
182 pp., 8 1/4 x 11 3/4 in., 170 pp. b/w photos and line drawings, paperback.
ISBN: 0-87040-383-4